Ska
An Oral History

T0055255

Ska

An Oral History

HEATHER AUGUSTYN

Foreword by Cedella Marley

McFarland & Company, Inc., Publishers
Jefferson, North Carolina, and London

LIBRARY OF CONGRESS CATALOGUING-IN-PUBLICATION DATA

Augustyn, Heather, 1972–
    Ska : an oral history / Heather Augustyn ; foreword by Cedella Marley.
        p.   cm.
    Includes bibliographical references and index.

    ISBN 978-0-7864-6040-3
    softcover : 50# alkaline paper ∞

    1. Ska (Music)— History and criticism.   I. Title.
ML3535.8.A84   2010   781.646 — dc22   2010036431

British Library cataloguing data are available

On the cover: (top from left) Lyn Taitt, facing camera (photograph by Greg Lawson); Stranger Cole (photograph by General Moses); (bottom, from left) Millicent "Patsy" Todd at microphone (photograph by Todd Campbell); Mighty Mighty Bosstones. (Taitt, Cole and Todd photographs courtesy of Steady Rock Productions, LLC)

Manufactured in the United States of America

McFarland & Company, Inc., Publishers
Box 611, Jefferson, North Carolina 28640
www.mcfarlandpub.com

For Ron, Sid, and Frank

Acknowledgments

To my brother, Charlie Ransford, for his undying encouragement, dead-on advice, and substantive guidance, without which this book could not exist (and for taking me to my first ska show).

To my mom, Linda Day, for her loving support.

To my dad, Chuck Ransford, for his interest.

To Barbara Funke, Carol Biel, Robert Kelly, James Ballowe, Kevin Stein, Richard Jones, John Scheibel, Pat Colander, and Julia Perla, for being my teachers, my mentors, and my internal audience, to whom I am always writing.

To my great friends, Amanda Petrucelli and Nikki Wood, for encouraging me through every trial and tribulation.

To fellow skamrade, Brad Klein, for his heartfelt assistance and kinship, as well as his additions to the book.

To Chuck Foster, with admiration, for his humorous advice and support.

To Brandon Kroft, for his generosity, counsel, and friendship.

To Robert Astle, for his professional assistance and support.

And to everyone included in this book, for your stories, your confidence, and your generosity.

And to Cedella Marley, for agreeing to write a foreword to this book, a special thank you is in order.

Table of Contents

Foreword
by Cedella Marley

in the beginning there was ska...

Before reggae there was rock steady, and before that, ska.

Everyone knows that, or should, by now. But never before *Ska: An Oral History* has the story been told by those who were actually there, creating the music.

My dad came into reggae his own way, with his own invention of sound squeezed out of the poverty and roots of music of all kinds — not just one kind. Ska was but one moment in the fast-moving zion train of linked events that made up his life. But it was a significant moment. I think a song like "One Cup of Coffee" is most typical of the early 1960s ska sounds that my dad developed in Trench Town while living in the house of Bunny Livingston's father.

When the stars and the moon and the wind were aligned just right, my dad could pick up far off American jukebox hits on his transistor radio. Songs like Brook Benton's "One Cup of Coffee" would come crackling through. Later my dad laid down a few tracks and "One Cup" was among them. I believe this may have been his first ska hit but others were "Terror" and "Judge Not."

My dad didn't see music timelines, as such. He heard rhythms, riddims, as we say in Jamaica. And these riddims were a little faster with ska, a blend of old calypso plus rhythm and blues. And they were a bit slower with rock steady. Finally, with reggae, the riddims slowed down even more as musicians brought in burra drums and the street beat of the Kingston ghetto, and the politics (politricks) of Jamaican life in general.

Much has already been said about the time, the music — how it all got going and how it goes on still. But this book is a rare one-of-a-kind look into the movers and shakers behind ska music. *Ska: An Oral History* is a worthy tribute to the days when the music was young, untried, and ready to make a big jump into the world's ear.

Cedella Marley is the daughter of Bob Marley, CEO of Tuff Gong International and the winner of three Grammy awards as a member of the Melody Makers.

Preface

EVERYONE WHO LOVES SKA has their own story to tell — the first time they heard the Specials back in the '70s, the first time they danced onstage at a Toasters show in the '80s, the first time they saw the Skatalites perform in the '90s. For fans of ska, they were the first to love it, the first to tattoo it on their arm, the first to have a scooter or a huge collection of original Jamaican 45s. There's a big sense of ownership and identity when it comes to ska music since so much of its creation is making the music one's own.

And so it is with the artists too. All claim to be the first to call the music ska, the first to play the ska beat, the first to have a number one record. But for the artists, laying claim to the music is even more personal, and even more troubling. It is disturbing to many of them how they could be the first to break ground in this strong musical tradition, have millions of fans who recognize their contribution and share their passion for their creative output, yet no one outside of that tight-knit group even knows their name.

When I first set out to write this book, I was a fan like all of the others. I first fell in love with ska after seeing Madness perform "House of Fun" on *The Young Ones*, that British import broadcast in the mid '80s on MTV. After that, I went to every ska show that came through Chicago. I put on my black and white checkered dress for every show and skanked with every rude boy and rude girl in the crowd. I bought everything I could afford in the Moon Ska catalog while working my way through grad school. My thirst for ska was insatiable. I wanted more, and better yet, I wanted to be informed, to know where this music came from, this music that could, with only a few notes, make me happy. Through my research, I was shocked to find there was little information about the origins of ska music. The Internet was still a new technology for the masses back in those days, but there was some information floating around about the Jamaican greats, documents other fans had created from their own experiences and liner notes, but hard cold facts were few and far between. While library bookshelves were amply filled with tomes on reggae or Bob Marley, where were the books on the music that gave birth to the artists and music that finally gained proper recognition? After all, ska music was more than just a precursor — it was a genre in its own right.

I decided it would become my work, my duty, to tell the story of ska music. But who was I? I was just a fan like all of the others. I knew then I had to be merely a conduit, a medium, through which the innovators could tell their own tales, and I would become the weaver of that rich tapestry. So I spent the next decade, even more, contacting these great artists, talking to them, in person, over the phone, listening to their experiences. Some were very willing to talk, relieved almost to recollect, and the conversations went on and on, like we were old friends, the artist and the fan. Others were reluctant and skeptical, wondering what I wanted and would I take advantage of their permission, because they had been taken advantage of before, time and time again. And that became the common thread, through the variations of the stories — how they began their career, how they started singing, how they found this form of music — through it all, the common thread, willing or reluctant, was that these artists, all of them, across the generations, across the world, with millions of fans — they never got their due.

As a journalist of many years I had had the pleasure of interviewing a great number of fascinating and interesting people, including Kurt Vonnegut just before his death; Sam Leach, the original promoter of the Beatles; a former director of the CIA, and heads of state in Asia. Never has anyone ever asked for money for an interview. But after the manuscript for this book was complete, one prominent artist, who had freely given me an interview, suddenly demanded an extravagant payment. If

I did not agree to it, he would not allow me to use his interview. Thus his interview is not found herein and will remain on a tape, dusty, in a box on my shelf.

For too long, greed was at the heart of the Jamaican music industry, and in some ways it is still alive and well. Several of these artists even talk about that experience, and it has been well documented outside of this book, and even made into movie plots. But I hope that I have been able to recognize these amazing artists in ways that celebrate their true value. Their worth is in the lives they have lived, and the contributions they have made to the world. "Up till now, I'm a poor guy," Skatalites chief musician and saxophonist Roland Alphonso told me backstage at their show in 1997 at the University of Chicago. I told him, "Yes, but you are a rich man," and patted my hand on my heart. "Aiyeee! Yes!" he responded. And that's why he continued to play until he collapsed on stage at the Key Club in Hollywood and later died, in November 1998. That's why Judge Dread literally sang his heart out, dying from a heart attack while performing at the Penny Theatre in Canterbury in March 1998. That's why Laurel Aitken, Tommy McCook, Desmond Dekker, Justin Hinds, Alton Ellis, and countless others performed until they died. What else could they do when they loved the music so?

This is why fans keep going to show after show, buying album after album — each claiming to be the first — because we love ska too. For the fans, to have ska stay underground is great. That's where it belongs so the music is not "sold out," so it's not corrupted by the whims and fickle ways of the mainstream where it would be morphed into something unrecognizable. But for the artists, at 70 years old, to have had hit record after hit record in their native country and still have the longevity, determination, and passion to spend all of the years of their lives on a tour bus and play with unparalleled skill for their fans and have nothing tangible to show for it, not even the recognition of their name outside of certain circles, well that's just a crime in a society that throws money at the latest pop tart.

Hopefully the present work pays just a little of the respect that is deserved to the greats who gave the world their talent and endless enthusiasm, influencing other musicians through the many ebbs and flows of ska over the generations. There are so many artists I couldn't talk to —

those who slipped away before I had the chance, or those who were reclusive or elusive in their later years. Let us not forget those musicians too and let this book, this conduit through which the artists speak to us, be a way to deepen our appreciation and love for ska music.

If the late historian Howard Zinn taught us anything, it's that history is made by those who are in power. Although there is no such political power here in the creating of this book, there is, in a way, a power of the spoken and written word. So those who are speaking this history, the musicians I interviewed, and those who are writing it, me and my sources of research, have created this single history. Especially with ska, with so many passionate fans and passionate artists, a sense of ownership means that a history can have many different versions. And especially because this is an oral history, it is even more a perspective, as is the nature of any history. But this is what, I believe, makes this history alive and interesting and dramatic.

So for those who do know ska's story, let this history be another view. And for those who don't yet know ska's story, let these artists' words be enlightenment that these men and women are great creators, tremendously skilled, and truly legends who deserve our admiration and awe.

CHAPTER ONE

Let the Good Times Roll: Derrick Morgan, with Millicent "Patsy" Todd and Lyn Taitt

B Y THE TIME SKA CAME TO JAMAICA, the country was ready for relief. Jamaicans were ready for music and good times that took reality away, if even for a night, out in a grassy lot, dressed to the nines, sweating and skanking to horns and fast syncopated rhythms from generator-run turntables, blaring through speakers on the back of a truck. Jamaica was a turbulent island, full of sunshine and tropical waves, but a land whose people continually battled colonization and stifling oppression. Much like the native peoples of America, Jamaica's early inhabitants were subjugated by the colonization that followed Christopher Columbus' arrival in 1494. The native people of Jamaica, a fishing, hunting, and agricultural people called the Arawaks, disappeared entirely seven decades after the arrival of Columbus. The Arawaks succumbed to the diseases of the Spanish conquerors, in addition to suffering from the rape of their wealth.

The next century and a half in Jamaica brought continued colonization from the Spanish, who used Jamaica primarily as a base for their conquest of the Americas and the plunder of the Americas' resources, namely gold and silver. But in 1655, the Spanish occupation came to an end with the British capture of the island. The British imposed oppression all their own upon the Jamaican people.

Because Jamaica's climate and habitat is conducive to growing sugar, the British capitalized on this market and for a short time employed indentured European labor on the sugar plantations. But, in the name of money and greed, the British soon began importing large numbers of slaves from Africa for labor. Britain prospered greatly on the backs of these slaves and Jamaica's entire economy and society revolved around the production of the sugar plantation. This continued until the mid-1800s, when the slaves were emancipated and the sugar plantations succumbed to the rise in the beet sugar market. The Jamaican economy diversified out of necessity and exports of coffee and bananas slowly rose. Former slaves became farmers in the years that followed emancipation, but struggles over land continued.

In 1938, during a time of great economic turmoil in the wake of the Great Depression, Jamaican sugar workers and dock workers rebelled against the oppressive economic conditions, inspired by organizer and national hero Marcus Garvey. From this rebellion emerged two political parties and their affiliated unions — the Jamaica Labour Party (JLP) and the Bustamante Industrial Trades Union, founded by Alexander Bustamante; and the People's National Party (PNP) and the National Workers Union, founded by Norman Manley. It was during this era of great upheaval that Derrick Morgan was born, during a time when the foundation for the country was being set, and during a time when music was king.

Derrick Morgan began singing when he was only three years old. He was born in Jamaica in the Stewarton district of a parish called Clarendon in 1940. He began singing around his house, making up his own songs. But at age three, Morgan's mother moved with him to Kingston to seek medical care for his developing blindness, which was caused by retina pigmentosis, a debilitating and deteriorating condition that led to his total blindness early in life. Morgan attended Kingston Senior High School and Maddle High School and continued to sing around his home and in church, where his father was a deacon. After graduating from school, Morgan became a bookkeeper, but soon decided to leave this line of work to pursue his dream. "I started at the age of 17 at a talent show in Jamaica at the Palace Theatre, by imitating Little Richard, singing 'Long Tall Sally' and 'Jenny Jenny' that night at the contest," Morgan says. That talent show was the *Vere Johns Opportunity Hour.*

Vere Everette Johns was a Jamaican postal worker who became a newspaper reporter, writing a music column each week for Jamaica's *Star* but he soon entered the world of radio and stage production. After living for a short time in the United States, and developing the concept of a talent show as a way to help a local theater boost its attendance and sales, Johns brought the idea — which had been the brainchild of his second wife, Lillian Margaret May — to Jamaica when they returned to reside. Johns's talent show took place at the Palace Theatre in Kingston. This venue was an outdoor theater, with seating at a price range to fit anyone's budget. Guests could reserve a premium box seat, or a wooden chair with a cushion under a roof, or they could sit out in the open air, but in full view of the stage, which was flanked by orchestra pits and at the base of a large movie screen. When the theater needed to supplement its movie income with another revenue stream, it held a talent show, and at these shows many artists got their start. Due to the open-air design of the venue, it was not unlike the sound system parties that also took place in the open, hot Jamaican nights — the simmering pot of musical styles from the Islands, from Africa, and from America. Almost anyone could afford to attend, since general admission was kept at only a shilling. Crowds began lining up early to attend the shows, which started at 8 P.M. each Wednesday night. Shows included not only musical acts, primarily singing, but also comedians, dancers, and even performers on bicycles. Talent shows became a popular form of entertainment and were also held at such locations as the Ambassador, the Ward, and the Majestic. Winners were selected based solely on audience approval — who received the loudest applause at the end of the night won the show. Needless to say, this form of selection allowed plenty of opportunity for corruption, such as packing the house with one's own friends or supporters, or paying off people to clap for a chosen artist. Sometimes after a performer won, audience members approached the winner in a threatening manner to demand part of the spoils. If a performer won or came in second place, they returned the next week to perform again, so the corruption continued. Like an early version of *American Idol,* winning the popular talent contests assured success in the musical circuit. Those who got their start through the *Vere Johns Opportunity Hour* include the great Desmond Dekker, Alton Ellis, John Holt, Dobby Dobson, Laurel Aitken, Lascelles Perkins, Jackie Edwards, Boris Gardiner, Bob Andy, the Wailers, and Derrick Morgan himself.

Morgan recalls his days at the *Vere Johns Talent Show* that led to his success:

> At the contest, I sang first [came in first place]. From there, there was a comedian in Jamaica called themselves Bim and Bam. They started taking me around doing stage shows. That was in 1957. The stage shows ride around and round and round until 1959. This man named Duke Reid, which is Trojan, used to ask some artists to do recording and I heard of it and went to him with two songs. I wrote one called "Oh My" and one called "Loverboy" and I asked him if he was interested and he said "yeah." He recorded those two songs for me and that's how I started recording, in 1959.

Recording was a hot business in Jamaica in the late 1950s and early 1960s. Only the rarest R&B tunes from America, or cheaper Jamaican-made tunes, were played at the sound system dances that took Kingston by storm. The dance was a gathering of Jamaican youth, dressed in the finest clothing, who came to hear the popular music and forget about the tough times. The dances were led by a sound system, a unit of large portable speakers that projected sounds from acetate discs. The speakers were enormous, called "houses of joy" because they were so big and powerful. The dances were held on concrete dance floors in open-air locations that were

Legendary ska vocalist Derrick Morgan helped launch the careers of numerous other Jamaican artists, including Bob Marley, Jimmy Cliff, and Desmond Dekker (photograph courtesy Derrick Morgan).

fenced off to contain the crowd. Food was sold nearby as vendors brought their carts of fruit or trays of hot jerk chicken or fried fish. Vendors in pick-up trucks sold crates of soda pop and bottles of Red Stripe or Heineken beer. The dances provided an escape from the difficult times in the Kingston ghetto. Lloyd Bradley, a sound system operator and author, aptly calls a sound system "the community's heartbeat." Many times the dances were located inside dancehalls, such as the Red Rooster, the Pioneer, or the Cho Co Mo, that included both indoor and outdoor facilities for thousands of dancers. Jamaicans could find a dance any night of the week and dance until morning came. The producer who had the best music drew the biggest crowds and reigned as king, an honor held in the highest esteem.

One of those producers, Arthur "Duke" Reid, was a tough man. He owned a liquor store called Treasure Isle Liquors that he and his wife Lucille began after she won the lottery. Reid always dressed in flashy suits and jewelry to flaunt his status, although it was said his success came also from his ties to organized crime in the U.S. and in Jamaica. He attracted attention everywhere he went, and demanded attention as well, wearing a crown on his head, a red cape trimmed in ermine, and he always carried two guns — a shotgun on his left hip and a .45 on his right hip with bandoliers crisscrossing his chest. When he came to DJ, his entourage lifted him high above their heads on a chair, or throne, for all to see, placing him at his post on the turntables which he played, gold rings on each of his ten fingers. He was known to fire his guns into the air at his shows in a show of his power and when he liked a song. He was also seen occasionally playing with a live grenade. His dances were held on the corner of Beeston Street and Pink Lane in the early days and then on Bond Street and Charles Street. When Reid arrived to spin discs, his fans would exclaim, "Here comes the Trojan," since his van in which he carried his equipment was a customized vehicle exported from England and made by Trojan Ltd., an auto company. Reid also founded his own radio program called "Treasure Isle Time," on the newly formed Radio Jamaica and the Rediffusion (RJR). He was a former police officer and used his connections with crime to defend his domain. He always was surrounded by his entourage, or thugs, who would "mash up" the opposition and strong arm anyone deemed a threat by cutting the electrical wires of their sound system, bashing speakers, and menacing the competition's crowds.

The main competition for Duke Reid was from Clement "Coxsone" Dodd. Coxsone was an operator of one of the most popular sound systems in Jamaica at the time called Sir Coxsone's Downbeat. Other DJs included Prince Buster, Count Boysie, Tom "the Great" Sebastian, Sir Nick the Champ, Count Smith the Blues Blaster, Bells, King Edwards, Skyrocket, V-Rocket, Admiral Comic, and Lord Koo's the Universe. Although Dodd liked to refer to himself as the Scorcher, he received the nickname Coxsone as a kid at the All Saints School where he played cricket. At the time there was a famous Yorkshire County Cricket Club cricket player named Alexander Coxon, and because Dodd was a good player, he received the nickname after Alexander Coxon with a British twist — Sir Coxsone (sometimes spelled Sir Coxson). Coxsone always loved jazz music and played his favorite artists, Dizzy Gillespie, Coleman Hawkins, Fats Navarro, and Charlie Parker, as a kid at his mother's liquor store, which was more like a bar, located on the corner of Love Lane and Beeston Street. Upon graduation, Coxsone worked as a carpenter building cabinets and traveled to the U.S., as many Jamaicans did, as migrant help in the sugar cane fields in the southern states. Here, Coxsone witnessed the popularity of American rhythm and blues first hand, instead of just hearing the sounds on Jamaican radio. Coxsone, seeing the opportunity, invested much of his wages in speakers, a turntable and receiver, and records of American R&B tunes, and shipped it all back to Jamaica, where he would build his career. He built his own speaker cabinets since he had the carpentry skills. He went on to found the legendary record label Studio One.

Competition between Duke Reid and Coxsone was fierce — so fierce, in fact, that many who remember Duke Reid during these years say they never saw him without his guns at his side. Morgan says he was strict about his business. When Morgan aligned himself with Reid, allegiance came to Coxsone's attention when he heard Morgan's new tunes.

> Duke Reid used to play "Loverboy" and "Oh My" and have a contest between me and a sound called Coxsone, Coxsone Dodd. They used to play contests among one another, but no one want to release any songs, so I leave Duke Reid and I do a song for Coxsone called "Leave Earth."

He didn't release it at all and was playing it against Duke Reid. "Leave Earth" and "Wigger Wee Shuffle" I give to Coxsone and used to play sound system war with them. From there I leave to this man called Little Wonder [a nickname given to producer Simeon L. Smith, after his sound system. He was also known as Hi-Lite, the name of his music store] and I record "Hey You Fat Man" [which] was my first release to the public and it went to number one. And then Duke Reid heard of it and when he heard about that song, he send some men to me, like they are bad men, and say I shouldn't have leave him and gone somewhere else. I went down to him and I start singing back for him, and this girl in my band called Millicent Todd, otherwise known as Patsy, do a song with me, "Love Not to Brag," and then we start to sing as a duet. We were the first duet in Jamaica [says Morgan].

Millicent "Patsy" Todd, performing at the Legends of Ska Concert at the Palais Royale Ballroom in Toronto on July 12, 2002. It was her first time on stage in 33 years (photograph by Todd Campbell, courtesy Steady Rock Productions, LLC).

Patsy got her start from Morgan in 1960 when she was only a young teenager. Patsy's mother, Miss Kitty, approached Morgan on Orange Street, although today Patsy says she has only heard the story from Morgan and didn't know the details.

Derrick told me the story because I didn't know anything about it. He said he saw this woman and she told him she had a daughter that could sing. And I saw this guy came to my gate, knock on my gate. I'm looking at him and he's saying he's Derrick Morgan, and I say to myself, "So?" And he said, "I heard you can sing," and I'm looking at him wondering what he's talking about. And he said, "Could you sing something for me?" and I said, "Why?" And he said, "I just want to hear something." And I did. But as far as I'm concerned, I didn't know who this guy was, what he wanted. Somebody just come appear to you, telling you he hear you can sing and if you would do a song with him. And at first I was kind of, something ain't right here. But then he told me a story about another artist that the song was about, and this guy, I hated him, still do. And when he said that, I was ready to sing that song. And I did. And we have this producer, Duke Reid, god rest his soul, a nice man, and he start shooting up the place. My god! I was so scared! I ran! And they said, "No! That's a good thing! When he hears something that he likes that's going to make a hit, this is what he does!" So that experience was great for me and after that it was history. The song was "Love Not To Brag."

The man who inspired the song was Monty Morris who grew up with Morgan and was known to be boastful. He and Morgan were vocal competitors.

Patsy says she had no formal vocal training but instead was naturally drawn to the art form.

I'm somebody who liked to listen to the radio, and I really got interested in this group, Frankie Lymon and the Teenagers. I used to hear them singing and I used to sing after them. It wasn't that I was growing up in a church with that kind of music because I was Catholic and it's just Latin they sing. But I loved music. For some reason I use music as a part of life. Music to me was, well it's really hard to say, but, people would say to me, "You are an entertainer, you never smoke, you never drink," and I would say, "No." And they would say, "But I don't understand. Everybody do," and I would say, "But I'm not everybody." But the thing they didn't understand was that music made me feel the way maybe how when they had their cigarette, or whatever they had, or their drink, it made me feel the same way. I feel like I was on cloud nine when I hear good music. And people would say, "You go to dance and you don't dance." "I don't have to dance to enjoy myself," and they would say, "You enjoy yourself?" And I say, "Yes." "But you didn't dance." I say, "That's not the point. The point is, there's something about music that can make me feel happy, it can make me cry, it can do a lot of things to me that would be very hard for you to do and you're not drunk or something." And that's how I look at music.

The process in the early days with Morgan was challenging, says Patsy, particularly because of her youth and because she was a girl.

It was hard. Very hard. I was 15, 16 years old. And it was hard because you didn't have a say. People would say, "I heard a song with you," or they would play it and say it's you and I say, "It is?" And I honestly don't know if it is because I didn't get the chance to go to rehearsal and things like that, and you listen to the band and the band rehearse with you and things like that. That's not what happened in our music. Our music, I would go to the studio and my partner would tell me, "This is so-and-so and so-and-so," and I would write it down, and I would sing from the paper, that was it. I don't remember what it was, what I did or how much record I did. I didn't have a say, to say to the musicians, "Would you play this," or "Would you play that." They would kill me. You just take what they give you and that's it. So music, if it's like now and I had the chance to do what I did before, it would have been much different because I could have said I wanted to play this or I wanted to play that. But it wasn't like this, you know? The musicians that we had were great musicians. I think they could play with anyone in this entire world. They knew music, they knew what they were doing. They were absolutely fantastic. But they were very egotistical. You know, it was either just them or nothing. The problem when you have a band that every musician in that band could be the leader, it's very hard. Because every man that was in the Skatalites, they could be the leader of the band. That's how great they were. They were great musicians. They were just plain rude people also. They didn't have any respect for anyone. That, I couldn't handle.

Working in tandem with Patsy on many songs, and also working solo, Morgan recorded for Prince Buster and Beverly's and created the bulk of his work. He kept recording through the changes in styles and the changes in tempo, but he never slowed down. Morgan recalls the way ska started: "Ska started by, well we are trying to make a rhythm and blues song. We were imitating songs from Louis Jordan, this kind of rhythm that they play. We imitating Louis Jordan, we imitating Smiley Lewis, Professor Longhair, Rosco Gordon." Other U.S. artists adored by Jamaicans include Dizzy Gillespie, Sarah Vaughan, Jimmy Reed, Bill

Doggett, Lloyd Price, Earl Hines, Nat King Cole, Billy Eckstine, Jesse Belvin, and the Moonglows. "These were the songs we were trying to make in Jamaica. When we didn't get the real blues style, we have a guitar strum that give a different type of sound. Guitar and the piano making a ska sound, like 'ska, ska,' that's why we call it ska. The sound of the guitar and the piano, that's why we give it the name ska," Morgan says. Guitarist Ernest Ranglin has described the difference between the R&B beat and the ska beat as *chink*-ka, *chink*-ka, *chink*-ka in R&B versus ka-*chink*, ka-*chink*, ka-*chink* in ska. Morgan also remembers his first meeting with Lyn Taitt:

> But we didn't like the name ska at the time, so we search for a name, a real name for Jamaican music. We love the ska, but this musician came down from Trinidad, called himself Lyn Taitt. He have a band called Lyn Taitt & the Jets and they came to Jamaica and this guitarist was Trinidad, but the rest of the players were Jamaican. Joe Isaac on drum and Lyn Taitt on guitar and Gladstone Anderson on piano and with this band, we were creating a new sound. We're trying to put a bass pattern against the music instead of playing standard string bass on straight, we use an electric bass now. With ska music we used to use string bass, a tall string bass. But we change it and the first song that [we] made in ska, we use this guy named Herman Sands. He was a pianist. He bring down an electric piano and play on "Blazing Fire." That was the first electric instrument of piano that play on ska music, was that electric piano. And this group called the Vagabonds, they had this player also who come down, and "Went to the Hop" was the first electric bass that play on ska music in Jamaica.

Nearlin "Lyn" Taitt was born in San Fernando, Trinidad, on June 22, 1934. He began playing music at a very young age and performed on the steel drums, or pan, in his native country, even winning prestigious competitions. But he soon changed to the guitar, at the age of 15, because of the stigma associated with steel drums. Taitt explains, "The steel pan was not accepted by the middle class or upper class at all. And I used to play the steel pan, so I tried to play guitar for my mother to accept me playing music." When Taitt was a teenager, he decided to make a career of his music. "When I get older, I left home. They sent me to Jamaica," he says. "They" is Byron Lee, the Jamaican musician and producer. Taitt came to Jamaica in 1962 to tour with his band, the Dutch

Brothers. "I heard of Byron's music in Trinidad. My band went to the Jamaican Independence to play with Bryon Lee all over the island in Jamaica. And my manager and them didn't pay us the money. So I stayed in Jamaica. It was a long time ago," recalls Taitt who also stood in for Jah Jerry in Studio One when the Skatalites recorded. Taitt's guitar style is similar to the sound produced by the steel pan he once mastered and has been described by many as "bubbling," a lively flavoring that gives tunes their spirit and energy.

Lyn Taitt (right), legendary Trinidad-born guitarist, performs at the Palais Royale Ballroom in Toronto in 2002. His bubbling style of guitar punctuated thousands of ska, rocksteady, and reggae songs. He died in 2010 after a battle with cancer (photograph by Greg Lawson, courtesy Steady Rock Productions, LLC).

Taitt moved to Toronto, Canada, in 1968, where he stayed for the rest of his days. "I have my own recording studio in my garage," he says, and he still plays guitar, collaborating with hundreds of artists over the years, including the Skatalites, Stranger Cole, Ken Boothe, and Joe Higgs. Taitt is perhaps most well known for his work with his band, Lyn Taitt & the Jets, and is credited with ushering in the genre of rocksteady. Influenced by his love for American music, he heard the change from R&B to soul and brought these sounds into his own music.

Morgan describes how these instruments, like Taitt's electric guitar and the bass and piano, led to the character and the evolution of the music that followed.

> From there we get the feel of the electric bass and we set a pattern to the bass playing, right? So by setting a pattern, the walking bass, which is the string bass, would play, which was a one without electric. We use an

electric bass to set a pattern which is how we get rocksteady now. The pattern of the bass slowed down the music and the piano and the guitar would strum a little slower and the drum would give off one, they call it one drop in Jamaica, so we get a one-drop beat and we call it rocksteady because at this time now in ska music, we used to spin. Hold the girl's hand and let her spin. But in rocksteady, you just rock to the beat. That's why we changed the name now from ska now to rocksteady. You have to remember, ska music is a foundation. What is ska? It is the guitar and the piano. That is what you call ska. And rocksteady is the same guitar and piano but it is the bass and the drum that changes and make it slower and we call it rocksteady.

Taitt, as an originator of the rocksteady sound, makes a clear distinction: "It's very simple. Ska is very fast. Rocksteady is very slow." He says his origins in Trinidad helped him to make the new Jamaican sound. "In my country there is fast calypso and slow calypso. In Jamaica only you had fast ska. So I say to myself, 'well, I will slow it down.'" The result was rocksteady, and the first rocksteady song was appropriately titled "Take It Easy," recorded by Lyn Taitt and Hopeton Lewis at Federal Recording Studio.

Morgan continues, "Still we didn't like the name rocksteady and we try for another one. 'Pop-a-top, pop-a-top,' you know? We tried that one but it did not last long. I only made 'Fat Man' with pop-a-top rhythm. It took off a little in England but it didn't last for long so we have to go ahead looking for another name."

Whether the transition between musical styles was as overt as Morgan says, or whether it was more organic and a reflection of the social fabric of the time, the point is that there were distinct musical styles created during this time in Jamaica that led to the emergence of reggae.

I have a brother-in-law named Bunny Lee, right? And while we were in the studio we were making rhythm, because I started Bunny Lee in the record business. That was in 1968. And while he was in the studio, he would say to the musicians, "Play reggae man! I would like you to play reggae!" So they ask him, "What is reggae?" and he would say, "Make the sound, reg'-gae, reg'-gae, reg'-gae." I would say Bunny Lee was the man that bring out that name. Everybody start calling this song reggae, right? And that's how we reached reggae. But we used to spell regga. And this guy from Trinidad send down some writing one day, but he spell reggae, right? So he write up ticket that way, so that's how reggae came about. Just by listening to the music we call it by that name [Morgan says].

The most well-known reggae artist of all time is Bob Marley, and like Morgan played a role in the start of reggae, he also played a role in the start of Bob Marley's career, as well as many other prominent artists.

When I was in Beverly's music, I met Bob Marley. I met him at a friend's house in Kingston, and she told him that I did recording and so on and asked if I could help him out, and I said, "Well meet me at Beverly's and we listen to his song there," and he came with a song called "Judge Not Before You Judge Yourself." We auditioned him, between Leslie Kong and myself, and that's how Bob got his start. We start Bob, we start Jimmy Cliff, we start Prince Buster, we start Desmond Dekker. I didn't start Toots because Toots came to me and I turned him down because I do auditions for Beverly's. Artists come to me and I audition them and that's how all of them get started by me. Desmond Dekker used to be my backup singer because he was with Beverly's for two years before he sang a song called "Honor Your Mother and Father," so while he was there, he was doing backup with me.

Morgan's career continued to thrive throughout the decades that followed. His popularity also grew in England, due in part to his presence there when the music found a new audience.

I go to England in '69 and I used to produce in England for this company called Palmer Records Company and produced "The Moon Hop" and I got linked with the skinheads in England and the skinheads really liked my songs and they took on to my songs very good. When I was in England, we would do different types of dances. We do ska, we do rocksteady there, we do reggae dance, and we do one called skank. We do all kind of dances. I do a lot of production for Palmer Records and do it all myself on Palmer Records. And I left and come back to Jamaica and do production for myself with Hop Records. I owned the label called Hop Records — my son and myself. My son called Courtney Morgan. There are many things that are happening for me in this last time because away from producing, I'm still doing a lot of shows all over. I do a lot in Europe and the U.S. — all over.

But it was when Morgan went to England that he and Patsy parted ways, all because of a misunderstanding and hurt feelings. Left alone in

Jamaica, Patsy was approached by another singer who offered her the opportunity to do duets once again. Patsy recalls,

Stranger [Cole] and I met, it was really funny. I was home again and the

gate always knocking because I lived beside Prince Buster. We lived beside each other. So every time they came to find Prince Buster they would be knocking on my gate and I'm getting upset. So I came out and I said to him, "Prince Buster is not here. This is not his house. That house is his." And he didn't come to see Prince Buster. He came to talk to me. I'm looking at him and said, "Why? I don't know you." So he said that Duke Reid sent him. And I said okay. And he said he wanted to do some record and the only way that Duke Reid would record him [was] if I sang with him. And it kind of hit me off guard because Derrick was in England, and I said to him, "I don't know about that, I have to think about it," and then I saw this guy really needed to do this. He believed he could make himself better and do something that he love and getting paid for it, you know, a charge was in him. And I said okay, I tell him yes. And that's how Stranger Cole and I came about and it really caused a friction because when Derrick came back from England, he figure to himself I couldn't wait. And we never talk to each other. And he went and sang with

Stranger Cole, photographed in February 2010 at the University of West Indies, Mona Campus. Cole performed with Patsy after her departure from Derrick Morgan. He went on to have a prolific career, recording hundreds of songs and collaborating with numerous artists (photograph by General Moses, courtesy Steady Rock Productions, LLC).

20

somebody else and I just went on my way and that's how we broke up. And he did not know at all and I said, "Do you really know what happened? You didn't ask. You didn't ask me anything," and I told him what it was. You know, it was so foolish, for two people went separate ways because of something that he didn't understand and he didn't ask, and I didn't think it was right for me to tell him why. And this is what happened with me and Derrick, why we split up. We were in different camps. He was with Duke Reid and Beverly's and I was with Tip Top, so we really never had anything where we'd see each other. And we had different stage shows, so we really weren't around each other.

Morgan felt challenged by Patsy's duets with Cole, so Morgan found other female vocal partners to record with out of spite, says Patsy. "It was bad because it was so funny to see something that was so simple. I was upset when I heard a song and somebody said to me, 'Oh, I just heard you and Derrick on the radio,' and I'm saying, 'I didn't sing anything with Derrick,' but when I heard it, I was just fuming, I said, 'How dare he,' not even thinking that I also did it, but do I know why I did it? I couldn't understand, but in his world, he was getting back at me for singing with somebody else. So he went and sang with somebody else. And that was really it. Just in November [2008], when I went down to Alton Ellis's funeral, that conversation came up and I tell him why," Patsy says. The other woman Morgan recorded with was Yvonne Harrison, who also recorded with Roy Panton when Millie Small (the duet of Roy & Millie) left for England as well. They recorded as Derrick Morgan & Yvonne and charted the hit, "Meekly Wait," the title taken from a gospel song. But the lyrics are very telling of the situation with Patsy, written by a man who was known for his overt challenges through song.

After her days with Stranger Cole, Patsy, like Morgan, did "go on" and left Jamaica too, but not for the promise of more musical fame. Instead, Patsy left Jamaica to leave her music behind forever.

> I could not take Jamaica anymore, the music. It was something you would see, and it's just not the artists and musicians, it's you make so many hits and you don't have anything to show for it. And one day, I just say I had enough. My manager, Sonia Pattinger, this woman, it was not about the money with her and me, because right now where I'm standing I think without her I wouldn't be here because she showed me what it was to be a lady. She showed me what to do in this world, how

to go about things and what she gave me, money couldn't buy it. So it wasn't really about the money with her, it was just that you've seen all of these things and you're wondering, what's really going on, because you're not getting ahead the way you think you should. It's sad to see that there are so much artists in that time, and not one of us, not one of us had a home of our own, a car of our own. Nothing. You know, so you wonder why am I doing this? And that's what it was all about.

I went to Belize with Byron Lee and they had some recording shop [studio] and when I went there, I wanted to get some orders for Miss Pattinger. And when I went there, I had three records on the chart, number one, number two, and number three. And it just blowed my mind. I am standing here with record number one, number two, and number three in their country and I don't have any money. And that day I decided when I go back to Jamaica, that was it. And I decided that if I stayed there, that's all I really knew how to do. And I called a friend of mine and I said I just want some time to think and she said, 'Why don't you come up?' and I came to America and I didn't go back. I didn't go back. That was it. That was in 1968. There's been a lot of ups and downs because I came, I was by myself. When I was in Jamaica it's not like I even lived by myself. I lived with my parents, so coming here, living with my girl-friend and her mother, it was kind of strange, but it's a choice I made. I figured to myself that if I went back, it would be showing that what I did, I had to turn back and I said come hell or high water I'm not going to do it. So I know I made a choice and the choice I made at the time, it was very hard because coming to America and you have no skill but what you left home with. The music here is totally different. Their music, their way of thinking, their this, their that, there's no way to know where to even start to get your foot in. So I was just saying to myself, 'Well this is it, this is your choice, you've got to stick with it.' As they say, you've made your bed, you have to lie in it. But fortunately, I was lucky that I got a job and I like it and I was there [Brooklyn, New York] until last year when, my mother is very ill and I have a brother who is mentally retarded and I said some-body has to take care of him, because she used to take care of him and she can't take care of him, so I decided to quit my job and come here [Florida] and take care of them, but I never thought that it was so hard that I couldn't do it, because Alzheimer's is not an easy thing. I was work-ing in a hospital in a cardio-care unit, the secretary there for the floor, and the people that we worked with, we were like family. In fact, they didn't even know the life I had before I came. Because that was my life. That was my personal business and I tell no one, so no one knew what I did.

Derrick Morgan may have had his legendary duo with Patsy, perhaps the first popular Jamaican boy-girl duo, but he also had a very adversarial dual musical relationship with Prince Buster, a competition that would produce some of the greatest music of this time.

Cecil Bustamente Campbell, better known as Prince Buster, was born in 1938 and was given his middle name in honor of Alexander Bustamante, leader of the Jamaica Labour Party. He was the son of a railway worker and was raised in a working-class family. He grew up on Orange Street in a rough neighborhood in Kingston and only ended up in the music industry after literally fighting his way in. He received the nickname "Buster" after his middle name, Bustamente, but "Prince" was the nickname he received while boxing. He learned the skill as a teenager from Jamaican boxing greats Kid Chocolate and Speedy Baker. He decided to leave boxing because he found there was no money to be made in it and instead began singing.

Music was always a part of Prince Buster's life. His grandmother was a devoutly religious woman and when Prince Buster visited his grandmother in the country, he experienced the songs of the church and singing during prayer time in his grandmother's home. Naturally, Prince Buster began to sing as well. In Kingston, Prince Buster was also surrounded by music, especially American rhythm and blues that was heard on radio broadcasts from New Orleans.

In late 1957 when Prince Buster won a game of street dice against two notorious men, Noel Jorse Jaw and Mean Stick, an argument ensued between Prince Buster and Mean Stick, who took Prince Buster's money at knife point. A week later, Prince Buster, also armed with a knife, returned the attack by hunting down Mean Stick and demanding back his money. Coxsone witnessed this exchange while walking down the street with one of his DJs, Count Machuki. Machuki was born Winston Cooper and is credited with being the first person to speak, or toast, over a record while it played. Machuki told jokes over instrumentals and performed a kind of ska skat which has become popular in ska music ever since. Sir Lord Comic's vocals in the Skatalites' song "Lucky Seven" are a prime example of the "heps" and "chicka chicka chicka" sounds that were precursors to rapping and beatboxing that came decades later. Other vocalists perform the voiced percussion with an effect like a katydid, rhythmically punctuating the song. After Machuki and Coxsone saw Prince Buster demand back his money, Coxsone asked Prince Buster to become his bodyguard at the sound system dances since they were so impressed that a 19-year-old would stand up to such a well known bad man. Machuki called Prince Buster "Wild Bill" and he was to collect money from people who attended the dance, spy on other sound system DJs, and prevent Coxsone's intruders from viewing the selections they were spinning at the dances.

In the late 1950s, Prince Buster used to play records at a hardware store owned by Tom "the Great" Sebastian. Tom's real name was Tom Wong. He was half Chinese-Jamaican and half African and he was known as a professional, never resorting to the rough and tough tactics of some of his contemporary DJs. He was one of the very first to have a sound system in the early 1950s that was located on the corner of Charles Street and Luke Lane. He eventually moved out of the competitive business of producing and opened up a fine club called the Silver Slipper but in 1971 he committed suicide.

While playing records at Sebastian's store, Prince Buster was approached by Coxsone who asked for his help. The association with Coxsone gave Prince Buster his entrance into the business, and his initial role was one of informant and protector. Prince Buster's charge was to help identify the musicians who performed on the competition's records at sound system dances. At first, before producers began recording local talent, they secured the finest rhythm and blues from excursions to the States. If a record had a label affixed to it, the producer immediately scratched it off to prevent the artist's name from being viewed by the competition's spies. Bribes for this type of information weren't uncommon. Prince Buster was one of those spies. But Prince Buster left work for Coxsone because he felt he wasn't compensated well and he longed for more money. He started his own sound system, the Voice of the People.

Prince Buster took the reins and tried to work the same methods he learned in his days with Coxsone, but instead found himself more in the studio than on the trade routes. Although he had intended to travel to America to secure the latest R&B records while employed by the farm work program, Prince Buster's plan didn't go as planned. Apparently, Prince

Buster was rejected to travel to the U.S. for farm work because the inspector noticed Prince Buster's hands were too mangled to perform such laborious work. His hands were damaged from his years spent as a boxer.

So Prince Buster turned to the wealth of local artists and claims it was during this time that he created the distinctive ska sound, a claim that many artists make. The music emerged as a synergy of artists and styles meshed with the culture of Jamaica for a recipe that could never be duplicated anywhere else at any other time. Prince Buster says that drummer and good friend Arkland "Drumbago" Parks, who was also a music arranger, was key to this process. He claims to have asked Drumbago to play a march, a style of song that he favored even as a young child. This march-style of music was popular in Jamaica as a form of celebration, protest, and even at funerals. He claims to have asked Drumbago to stress the beat on the one and the three counts, instead of the traditional two and four counts. He contends that he asked Jah Jerry to perform a guitar strum and Dennis Campbell to perform a saxophone syncopation to accent the rhythm, and the sound of ska was born.

Prince Buster's boxing start and street tough carried through his entire life, and never was that combative spirit more apparent than in his very public battle, in a competition in song, against Derrick Morgan, which began in 1962, the same year Jamaica gained its independence. Morgan had left Duke Reid and begun working with Leslie Kong, another producer in Jamaica, better known as Beverly's. He recorded such artists as Jimmy Cliff, Toots Hibbert, and "Bobby Martell," the pseudonym under which Beverly's marketed Bob Marley (sometimes even misspelled as Bob Morley). Morgan says he first knew of Kong not as a producer, but as a restaurateur.

"I knew Beverly's but I didn't know them as recording people. They only own a restaurant at the time called Beverly's Restaurant. They weren't doing recording. But it seemed they wanted me a long time and didn't know how to get in touch with me," says Morgan. But there was a person who did know how to find Morgan, and one day in 1961, that liaison approached Morgan. "One day while I was home, this boy came to me and said he had a song called 'Dearest Beverly' and these people at Beverly's sent him to me and I was to listen to that person, and that boy I am talking about was Jimmy Cliff. He said I was to listen to him and if I like this song he will take me back with him to meet Beverly. Jimmy sang a song called 'Dearest Beverly.' It was a ballad and I listen to Jimmy. His right name is James Chambers and we give him the name Jimmy Cliff after he start making hits in Beverly's. So Jimmy Cliff went to Beverly's and I met this man called Leslie Kong."

Leslie Kong owned and operated a restaurant and ice cream parlor on Orange Street in Jamaica. Kong remodeled his restaurant to contain a recording studio on the premises and he recorded many of Jamaica's greatest artists, including Jimmy Cliff, Derrick Morgan, Desmond Dekker, Toots and the Maytals, Drumbago, Roland Alphonso, Ken Boothe, Peter Tosh, and Bob Marley and the Wailers. Kong died in 1971 of a heart attack, after Peter Tosh supposedly put a curse on Kong for releasing the album *The Best of the Wailers* before the Wailers believed they had produced their greatest work. Kong was only 38 years old at the time of his death, but in his short life he was responsible for launching the careers of many of the greatest Jamaican musicians, and building a great body of work from Derrick Morgan.

"He [Kong] tell me all of Jimmy's songs sound great. We wrote a song called 'Hurricane Hattie' with Jimmy and he ask me if I would do some songs for him too, and I said sure," says Morgan. But Morgan was also working with Prince Buster at the same time, collaborating on writing songs as well as recording songs, including "They Got to Go," in 1962. Morgan remembers the details and says his decision was based on money and autonomy. "When we did those songs on Beverly's, he paid me better than the rest. Duke Reid used to pay ten pounds. Prince Buster paid ten pounds. But Beverly's, which is Leslie Kong, was paying twenty, so I stick with him, and I had been with Beverly's a good while making hit after hit. Being with Beverly's, I didn't sign a contract. I could sing for anyone else, but I stick more with Beverly's and made more songs there," he said. Getting paid for a song was not the same business as today. There were no royalties, no fees, no licensing. Instead, artists received a flat fee to make the record, and since many artists had families and wanted to make a living from singing, the amount of pay was even more critical.

The feud with Prince Buster started because of Morgan's choice to record with Beverly's instead of Prince Buster. Morgan says, "In 1962 now, I made this one, when Jamaica was getting independent, I wrote a song called 'Forward March,' getting to the independence, and it was a big sellout. It was a boom. And on the Independence [Day], we on the truck [sound system] going around singing that song 'Forward March' and so on, and it was so good that Prince Buster getting jealous. He started saying that I took his belongings and take it to the Chinese man, because Leslie Kong was a Chinese, so I don't know what belongings he was talking about. Not until years later do I find out what he's talking about."

Morgan explains the source of the discontent — the claim of a stolen musician. "There's a song called 'They Got to Come.' The first one they made was 'They Got to Go.' And this was a song, 'They Got to Come.' Lester Sterling from the Skatalites take a solo for that song and he blow the wind instrument and when he do that solo now, Prince Buster, in my song called 'Forward March,' it was blow by an alto sax named Headley Bennett. Bennett blows very close to his one in 'They Got to Come,' so that's how he claimed I took his belongings to the Chinaman and he called it 'Blackhead Chinaman,' and I keep bucking and call it, tell him must walk the 'Blazing Fire,' and that was a bigger seller than him," says Morgan. Prince Buster's "Blackhead Chinaman" was banned by RJR, Radio Jamaica because of its racist content. It was a direct racist insult against Kong, Morgan's producer.

A refrain from Morgan's "Blazing Fire" replies back to Prince Buster's "Blackhead Chinaman":

> You said it I am a Blackhead Chiney
> But be still and know I'm your superior.
> Time is longer than rope [a reference to another of Prince Buster's songs]
> And time no catchin' up on you.
> You said it, so walk a blazing fire.

Each responded in kind, back and forth in song, such as "Praise and No Raise," "No Praise No Raise," etc. And then another series of songs between Prince Buster and Derrick Morgan followed, fueled by a competitive battle. A major part of the Prince Buster and Derrick Morgan rivalry came through their rude boy and Judge Dread songs that not only were a call and response to one another, but also acknowledged the violence of the day. "In the '60s there were some bad boys, they call themselves 'rudies.' Those guys would try to hurt anyone who came close to them. That's how I made 'Tougher Than Tough,' which is 'Rudies Don't Fear,'" says Morgan.

Morgan describes a personal run-in with one of these rude boys, a notorious criminal named Busby.

> I originally came out with a song called "Cry Tough," and this rude guy who call himself Busby, he heard of it and he come to me one day. He used to come around often when we living in Greenwich Farm. They come to me and said, "Well I want you to make a song after me. You make sure to make a song off of me and I want it Friday." We were afraid of him. So I said, "What kind of song you want me to make of you," and he said, "You sing of me," and I said, "Okay, well I will make you one," and I go ahead and I write a song called "Rougher Than Rough" and I go to Leslie Kong with it and I said, "Leslie, this bad man threaten me to bring a song to him and I will write a song of him and to come back Friday," but Leslie Kong said, "Well we can't release a song by Friday.' He said, 'Do you have the song ready?" I say yes and I used to play piano around there and I go around playing this song, "Tougher Than Tough" that I wrote in Beverly's one day and I said, "Ready. We will go to the studio Friday." And we cut the acetate on Friday and I took it to the guy and I said, "This is your song," and we're having a dance right there in Greenwich Farm that night on West Avenue, and he was going to play it that night to hear its sound. So that night he took the song from me and he gave it to the disc jockey and said he don't want to hear it play until twelve in the night. And at twelve o'clock in the night this rude boy went to the man and said, "Well okay, I would like you to play my song now." And when it reached the part that said, "Rougher than rough, tougher than tough, strong like lion, we are iron," he said, "Stop it there! Sell me a box of beer," and I give him a box of beer, and to play back the song. And then we go with him and the beer to the back and he crash it against the wall and said, "Iron!" and get rough.

The song featured the legendary vocalist Desmond Dekker on harmonies and Morgan spoke at the beginning of the song's instrumentals, declaring:

> You're brought here for gun shooting
> Ratchet using, and bomb throwings.
> Now tell me rude boys, what have you say for yourselves?

The response came:

Your honor, rudies don't fear.

The incident made Morgan's song a hit and when it would play on juke-boxes around Jamaica, drinkers smashed their beers on the wall upon hearing the words, "Strong like lion, we are iron." The song was therefore banned from radio play.

And the song sparked one final act of violence, upon that rude boy Busby himself. "This guy that was getting out of hand now that song been made and him get worse, say rudies don't fear. Every jukebox in Jamaica was playing it then. And this guy that I wrote the song for, he listen to this song that night and go on with his antics. That was a Friday night and he died on the Saturday night. They shoot him on Saturday night. He was bad. That song really really takes him to the graveyard," says Morgan. Busby was shot in the head by a rival gang member while at a party.

But the song sparked another rivalry as well — the rivalry between Morgan and Prince Buster. "Prince Buster made this song called 'Judge Dread' because when I made the song, 'Tougher Than Tough, Rudies Don't Fear,' he made one after that named 'Judge Dread,' said he was going to put rudies in court, and that's how we start to make Judge Dread. They have a guy down there saying rudies don't fear, but my name is Judge Dread and I don't care. He give 'em a hundred years. He's Judge Dread. When Prince Buster start making Judge Dread, then I put Judge One-Hundred Years and do some judge songs because the audience like it. People like those songs," he says. Rude boys may be considered a novelty or an icon of ska music today, but in the 1950s and 1960s in Jamaica, a rude boy was a gangster, no less fearsome than today's gangsters. And although some of them may have had a life of petty crime, still others, like Busby, were true psychopaths. Prince Buster says it was after an incident in West Kingston where a rude boy broke into a school, raped a school girl, and battered and assaulted her teacher that he created the Judge Dread mythical character, to portray the rude boys in the appropriate negative light. The persona was an attempt to restore social order, says Prince Buster. Judge Dread sentenced the rude boys, regardless of their pleas for mercy and even crying, to such unreasonable sentences as 400 years.

Derrick Morgan (right) performs with Prince Buster. The two have had an ongoing musical war since they began singing in Jamaica in the 1960s (photograph courtesy Derrick Morgan).

Other songs in this vein include Derrick Morgan's "Court Dismiss" and "Cool Off Rudies" and Prince Buster's "Johnny Cool," "the Barrister," and "Judge Dread Dance (the Pardon)." The dispute between rudies and Judge Dread ended with Morgan's humorous song, "Judge Dread in Court," where Morgan jails the jailer for impersonating a judge. Numerous other artists were inspired by the fictional trials and recorded rude boy and Judge Dread songs of their own.

"That's how we started fighting. It was friendly," Morgan says now, but at the time, it was anything but friendly for the fans of Morgan and Prince Buster. "'Blazing Fire' and 'Judge Dread' and all these songs where we knock one another—it became personal in Jamaica in that time because we both have fans. Buster have fans and I've got fans. The fighting, they start taking it too personal. All who like Derrick would say Derrick better than Prince, and all who like Prince would say Prince better, and this caused fights," says Morgan. The fans of Morgan and Prince Buster were members of street gangs who broke out in violent

Derrick Morgan and Millicent "Patsy" Todd on stage prior to performing "Look Before You Leap" at The Legends of Ska Concert, July 12, 2002, at the Palais Royale Ballroom in Toronto. It was the first time the duo sang together in 37 years (photograph by Greg Lawson, courtesy Steady Rock Productions, LLC).

fights, and in bars in Kingston, men fought and cut each other with knives in disputes over the two singers. Prime Minister Hugh Lawson Shearer, in order to quell the violence, decided to step in and he approached the *Jamaica Gleaner*, the biggest newspaper in the country, for help. "What we do is we get together and go into the paper and hug up and take pictures together that we're friends and this keep down the violence. So we did this and cooled down and cut out the songs singing off of one another," says Morgan.

But Morgan admits that photograph was staged to prevent violence in Kingston. And Morgan says the rivalry was not so friendly below the surface, despite attempts to bring the two together. "We toured England together in 1963, Prince Buster and myself, and we only do a few songs. We do no march because it was a jealously business from Prince, where I don't know his reason. To me, he was very jealous of me. I don't know, but the first time we did a show, one in London and one in Brixton, and the one we did in Brixton, Prince Buster would pay some guys to try and booing me, but it didn't work out. They turned around and booing him. He was envious," Morgan says.

For Derrick and Patsy, Jamaica's first couple of ska, a misunderstanding and the years may have kept them apart, but they were reunited onstage at the Legends of Ska concert in July 2002, at the Palais Royale Ballroom in Toronto, Canada. It was Todd's first time on stage in 33 years. But she says she has no regrets over leaving the music business and feels that the great artists of her day never got their due:

> I know that the music itself has done a lot, really, worldwide. For an island to do what we did, you know, it's great. The thing that really kind of upset me sometimes, that I see men like Alton Ellis, Ken Boothe, Stranger [Cole], Derrick [Morgan], all of these guys, they worked their soul. Their soul and everything was in this music and you wonder, what for? What did they really get? What did they accomplish? It's very hard to see it because in America you'd have a hit song and you could live for the rest of your life on that money for whatever you need. We have hundreds and hundreds of hit songs. It didn't do anything. Delroy Wilson, people like that, died from being heart broken or whatever because they didn't accomplish their dream or what they needed in life.

Millicent "Patsy" Todd (left) and Doreen Shaffer (right) backstage immediately following Todd's performance with Derrick Morgan at The Legends of Ska concert, July 12, 2002, at the Palais Royale Ballroom in Toronto (photograph by Greg Lawson, courtesy Steady Rock Productions, LLC).

When asked if she sings anymore, she replies,

No, I don't. From 1968 I never sang anymore, I never did anything like that. Derrick Morgan always said, "Why don't you come back out, why don't we make some music," and I said no. But it was so strange, I was watching Bob Marley on the television and I'm looking at this guy and I said, "This guy is dead, and it's like he's alive, sitting there, talking." If I didn't know he was dead, I would think this was someone alive. And I thought at least for the generation to come, people will see and hear about Jamaican music and know what it's all about. Looking at it now and what's going on now, we have a lot of Jamaican guys and women or whatever and sometimes I wonder to myself, do they realize that we paved that part? We didn't get anything but we paved that part for them, and I don't think they know that. And I don't think they would get it because they think this is "now time" and the "this time," and the "that time," but if it wasn't for your grandmother, your mother wouldn't be here, and if it wasn't for your mother, you wouldn't be here, so it has to come from somewhere. It's sad. Derrick had in Jamaica three or four hits straight on the chart, one, two, three, four. This guy don't have any money that he should have. And I don't understand. There are so few artists from my time that are still in the business. These are new guys singing new records, and their thing is different from ours, but I don't care what they say, I would put ours to theirs and they can forget it.

CHAPTER TWO

Queen of Ska: Doreen Shaffer with Lloyd Knibb, Lloyd Brevett, Roland Alphonso and Lester Sterling

S HE TAKES THE STAGE in her tropical print baseball hat and turquoise shirt as the crowd, fans ranging in age from 15 to 50, erupts in wild applause and hoots of appreciation. She smiles sweetly and removes the microphone from its stand, ready to give the people what they want. Backed by the legendary Skatalites, this is Doreen Shaffer, and she sings "Simmer Down," the same song they wrote and played for the young Bob Marley decades ago, the first time he recorded at Studio One in Kingston.

Doreen Shaffer was born Monica Johnson in Kingston, Jamaica, and grew up in a home where singing was a part of everyday life. Her father was German and her mother Costa Rican, and her mother was an inspiration for Shaffer's future as a vocalist. "My mama, I would hear her singing when we go to church and she was always singing around the house. But there was no music around of such, no music of such, say like somebody was in that field. So I started singing at school a lot. I did a lot of school plays and like that. In Kingston, Jamaica, I went to elementary school, and when I leave school there I went on to night school at Durham College. I don't know if it's in existence anymore. So that's where it really started for me, singing around classmates and they would say, 'You should sing.' I grew up with that in the back of my mind. That's a project I'm going to get involved in," says Shaffer. "But I actually went to school for business."

Shaffer enjoyed singing the songs performed by her favorite American jazz artists, such as Dinah Washington and Sarah Vaughan. And like many Kingston musicians in the 1960s, Shaffer got her start in Studio One recording for Clement "Coxsone" Dodd. It was here she met and recorded duets with singer Jackie Opel. And it wasn't long before she met and joined the rest of the members of the legendary group, the Skatalites, as one of their vocalists, along with Opel and Lord Tanamo.

The Skatalites formed in 1964 but they had already been performing together for years as the session musicians, or backing band, to almost all of the vocalists who came through Studio One.

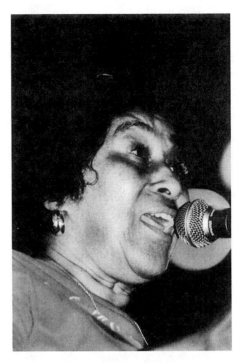

Queen of ska, Doreen Shaffer, performs with the Skatalites in Chicago in 1997. Her classic tunes include, "You're Wondering Now," "Sugar Sugar," and "Simmer Down" (photograph Heather Augustyn).

Everyone from Derrick Morgan to Prince Buster to the Wailers used members of the Skatalites to back their hits, and in between recording sessions, the group wrote and performed their own music, composing such classics as "The Guns of Navarone" (a ska adaptation of the theme song to the hit movie of the same name) and "Eastern Standard Time." These songs are perfect evidence of the jazz training and instructional background each of the musicians possessed, and without which they would not have had such success.

The Skatalites were named first by Lord Tanamo, and were called the Satellites, since it was the same week as the launch of a Soviet satellite during the space race. But Tommy McCook, leader of the group, jokingly suggested the Skatalites as a witty alternative, and it stuck. The group was comprised of saxophonist Tommy McCook, tenor saxophonist Roland Alphonso, alto saxophonist Lester Sterling, trumpeter Johnny "Dizzy" Moore, drummer Lloyd Knibb, guitarist "Jah" Jerry Haynes, keyboardist Jackie Mittoo, vocalists Doreen Shaffer and Jackie Opel, bassist Lloyd Brevett, and trombonist Don Drummond. And in the traditional style of jazz, the Skatalites frequently performed their recorded and live songs with an introduction of the song's theme, a variation on that theme performed by each soloing musician, and then at the end of the song, they returned to the main theme.

Tommy McCook was born in 1927 in Havana, Cuba, and was not only a saxophonist, learning to play from a very early age, but he was also the bandleader of the Skatalites and founder of the group. McCook, like many great Jamaican instrumentalists, attended the Alpha Boys School in Kingston. The school was for the underprivileged children of Kingston and provided them with a Catholic curriculum and a rigorous music foundation. The school employed a strict, many times corporal form of discipline. The school's music program mentor and spiritual guide was Sister Mary Ignatius Davies, who worked at the school from 1939 until her death in 2003. The school was founded by Justina Ripall in the 1880s and part of the school served as an orphanage. Alpha Boys School provided stability and routine to boys with potential but without means. In the 1940s and 1950s, the music school, under Sister Mary Ignatius Davies' tutelage, flourished. Students studied traditional curriculum for half of the day and music for the other half of the day, and because so many students attended, competition for use of the school's few instruments was fierce. Other Alpha Boys School alumni include Vin Gordon, Winston Foster (Yellowman), "Deadley" Headley Bennett, Cedric "Im" Brooks, Johnny "Dizzy" Moore, Lester Sterling, Glen DaCosta, Floyd Lloyd, Joseph "Jo Jo" Bennett, Bobby Ellis, David Madden, Rico Rodriguez, Owen Gray, Don Drummond, Leroy Wallace, Tony Greene, Johnny Osbourne, Leroy Smart, Tony Gregory, Ron Wilson, Raymond Harper, and Eddie "Tan Tan" Thornton.

McCook, who grew up without a father, attended the Alpha Boys School because his mother struggled to keep the family afloat. The school trained students to perform music so they could attain income-producing jobs in Jamaica's tourist industry after graduation. And McCook did just that, finding employment in hotels as an instrumentalist with the Eric Dean Orchestra. The group performed big-band style music that was brought from America to Jamaica via the radio airwaves. The sounds of Count Basie and Duke Ellington were popular with McCook and the musicians of his day.

Alpha Boys School emblem.

McCook also gained musical knowledge when he lived in the Bahamas from 1954 to 1962, and there his love and skill of jazz was further honed. McCook continued to perform in this jazz/big band style, even into the ska era, and when the ska rhythm, produced by percussion, guitar, and keyboard, was added, the result was contagious. McCook performed with the Skatalites for the months they were together from the spring of 1964 to August 1965 when he left the group. He re-formed the group for a reunion at the Sunsplash Festival in Montego Bay, Jamaica, in the summer of 1983. McCook continued to perform with the band from 1986 when they re-formed again, until he suffered a heart attack in 1995, although he did still record with the band in the studio after this setback. McCook died on May 5, 1998.

Another graduate of the Alpha Boys School was Lester Sterling, alto sax player for the Skatalites. Sterling, like many other young students, attended the Alpha Boys School as a way to turn music into a business and develop a passion for the arts. "I went to Alpha Boys School. It was nice. It was preparatory for music and other things, trade school. Sometimes I look back at my school days and the music they were teaching me and it was so advanced. They were talking about major and minor scales and chromatics and everything to begin with," says Sterling.

Sterling originally learned to play the trumpet, and like many other members of the Skatalites, he played multiple instruments. Sterling played the trumpet in many other bands, as well as the flute and piano, before settling on the saxophone as his instrument of choice for the Skatalites. He was introduced to Coxsone and the group by Rico Rodriguez who asked Sterling to accompany him to an audition one day. "I was the trumpeter. My original instrument was trumpet. We play together. Then the business started. That's when I switched instruments," Sterling says. Sterling says he got to know members of the Skatalites and other musicians from running in the same circles. "Three guys were like teenage friends. Young musicians, we were living together, and that was before the Skatalites. Myself and Lloyd Brevett and Rico Rodriguez, trombone. So we used to play at the local clubs. We were playing the popular music. Fats Domino type of music, bluesy-like, you know?" Fats Domino performed in Jamaica in early 1961, making an impression on the citizens.

Lester Sterling, alto saxophone player for the Skatalites, performs in Chicago in 1997. Sterling claims to have started reggae with his song, "Bang-a-rang" (photograph Heather Augustyn).

Sterling says he remembers the days in the studio playing with the original members of the band and says they were the ones who set the stage for those who followed. "When we were practicing in Trenchtown, we were there before Bob Marley. We practiced everyday there. Everyday we had to practice. At that time, Rita Marley was around. She used to come up and stand and look at us, like she don't want to go to school, and avoid ten minutes. Rita Marley in her school uniform. At that time, Bob Marley wasn't around. I knew Bob well," Sterling says.

After playing with the Skatalites in 1964 until their initial breakup, Sterling went to play trumpet for Byron Lee and the Dragonaires. "I was the trumpeter for Byron Lee and the Dragonaires. In the '60s after the Skatalites, I was in his band as a trumpeter. I spend five years," says Sterling. Byron Lee and the Dragonaires was a band that had debuted the ska sound, and ska dance, now known as the skank, to the rest of the world at the 1964 World's Fair in New York City. The skank, according to Timothy White in his book, *Catch a Fire*, has its origins in Rastafari culture. "Dreads would sit on their haunches in tight circles, passing the chillum pipe, a clay hookah with an 'unskanked' (unbent, hence the name of the dance step) six-inch tube," writes White. Because the skank was a dance where dancers bent themselves with the rhythm, it was called the skank. The dance was debuted by Ronnie Nasralla and Jannette Phillips at the World's Fair. Nasralla went on later to manage Byron Lee and the Dragonaires. The dancers introduced the "Backy Skank," the "Rootsman Skank," and the "Ska," since it was popular to name dances in American during the day (Mashed Potato, Twist, Stroll, etc.). Other artists presenting Jamaican music to the rest of the world at the 1964 World's Fair in New York City, backed by Byron Lee and the Dragonaires, were Jimmy Cliff, Prince Buster, Monty Morris, and Millie Small.

The selection of Byron Lee and the Dragonaires for this slot was never forgiven by the Skatalites nor the fans of the Skatalites, who knew that the band had been snubbed. When the Jamaican Government, in order to promote tourism to the island, chose to send a group of musicians to introduce the newly created ska sound to the world, selecting those musicians was a political decision rather than one based upon skill or success. Edward Seaga, the Jamaican Minister of Development and Welfare, was named to the Legislative Council of the Jamaican Parliament in his days before becoming leader of the Labour Party and Prime Minister of Jamaica. Seaga had previously been owner of Federal Studios, WIRL Records, and more importantly, was manager to Byron Lee and the Dragonaires and sold WIRL Records to Lee in the mid–1960s. Hence, Seaga essentially chose his own band to represent the country. Lee was sent by Seaga, who had a love for Jamaican culture having studied the Jamaican-African religions of Kumina and Pocomania in graduate school, to the Kingston ghettos to investigate this music that was seeping out of impoverished towns into the dancehalls and the clubs patronized by tourists. Because Lee was accepted by the middle classes, he became Seaga's messenger of the music his constituents loved. Seaga's nickname became Ska-aga, in recognition of his affinity for the music.

But Jackie Mittoo, keyboardist for the Skatalites, claimed that their band of musicians was intentionally not chosen for the position since some of their members smoked ganja. Even Coxsone denounced the selection of Byron Lee and the Dragonaires to the World's Fair, claiming the purpose of bringing a band was to educate the world on ska, but instead they were sending a group that knew nothing of the genre. And time has proven the critics correct, since the Skatalites have continued to spread the ska culture to the world ever since.

With talent so profound, it is stunning to think the Skatalites were originally together for a little more than one year. A contributing factor to why the band fell apart in 1965 was due to the difficulties, and ultimate tragedy of the life of one of the Skatalites' most important musicians, trombonist Don Drummond. Drummond was born in Kingston in 1932. He too learned to play music at the Alpha Boys School and was such a great talent that he even returned to teach younger students. He left the Alpha Boys School six weeks early to perform for the Eric Dean Orchestra in 1955. He then formed his own group, The Don Drummond Four, as well as other groups such as Tony Brown's Orchestra with other Alpha Boys School students. Drummond frequently performed at the Majestic Theatre and recorded one-offs for Coxsone after he discovered Drummond performing there. One-offs, or specials, were one acetate disc of a recording. In the early days, recording studios, which were typically located in a spare room in businesses or night clubs, only had the capability of producing one acetate disc and never more than one or two hundred as there was simply no market for the records since few to whom the music appealed could afford a record player.

Drummond was a fantastic composer and arranger and wrote many of the Skatalites' songs, such as "Eastern Standard Time," "Schooling the Duke," and "Man on the Street." He was a devout Rasta and frequently visited Count Ossie's Camp where he learned from other musicians and influenced countless others, such as Rico Rodriguez. But there was a dark side to Drummond that many who played with him saw from time to time. He was very strictly disciplined and tended to keep to himself in quiet bouts of reclusion. Even before joining the Skatalites, Drummond underwent a treatment program for mental illness at a local facility. It was one of many visits Drummond would make over the years as he battled manic depression that he regulated himself, in a largely misunderstood era for mental illness, by using large amounts of marijuana to stay balanced. He was later diagnosed as schizophrenic. Still, Drummond wrote and recorded music prolifically. He was a creative genius and produced numerous hits for Coxsone at Studio One and the members of the Skatalites.

But on New Year's Eve, 1965, Don Drummond's girlfriend, Anita "Marguerita" Mahfood, a dancer known professionally as "Marguerita the Rhumba Queen," wanted to dance, which she did, at the Baby Grand and at Club Havana. Many contend that Drummond was not keen on his live-in love's occupation and he forbade her to go. To get her way, Marguerita gave Drummond his medication late, causing him to fall asleep and miss a performance with the Skatalites at the Parisienne Club in Harbour View. When Marguerita returned at 3:30 in the morning, an argument ensued that ended in violence. Constable Aston Pennycooke of the Rockfort Police Station saw Drummond walk into the facility and exclaim, "A woman in the yard stab herself with a knife and I would like the police to come and see her," according to police records. When the police arrived, they found Marguerita stabbed multiple times, dead on the floor, her hand pushed into the bell of Drummond's trombone, possibly her way of indicating the murderer to investigators in her final moments of life. "Don Drummond killed Marguerita, his girlfriend," remembers Lloyd Brevett. She was not only Drummond's girlfriend, but she also sang vocals for the Skatalites on their song, "Woman A Come," which Marguerita wanted to name "Dunga Gun Malungu" but Duke Reid changed it.

The coroner ruled that the knife wounds could not have been self inflicted and in the subsequent trial, Drummond was found guilty of Marguerita's murder. He was remanded to the Bellevue Asylum and there he was found beaten to death four years later in 1969. He was buried in an unmarked grave in Maypen. His death was ruled a suicide, although some members of the Skatalites and others say Drummond's death could not have been suicide. Some contend he was beaten to death by guards at the asylum as a way for the Jamaican government to quell the music scene and Rasta culture, an effort keenly detailed in Timothy White's *Catch A Fire: The Life of Bob Marley*. Others feel that Marguerita's father may have ordered a retaliatory hit on Drummond at the hands of connected gangsters.

Drummond's death was devastating to the Skatalites. Drummond was such a ravenous composer that by the time of his death, at only the age of 27, he had written over 300 songs. McCook said Drummond could turn a simple song into a gem, and without this creative force, the Skatalites fell apart and members went their separate ways. This death, combined with inadequacies in Coxsone's payments to the Skatalites, created strife among the band members who all were very independent musicians with their own agendas, schedules, and concerns. "I decided to quit because this guy not paying what we want him to. We couldn't get it, so we had to stop playing. And Drummond was the highlight of the band," says Brevett. McCook left the band in August 1965, and the rest of the band chose not to go on without him.

One musician who thrived, both as a member of the Skatalites and in the years after the band's initial breakup, was Roland Alphonso. Born in Havana, Cuba, on January 12, 1931, Alphonso came to Jamaica with his mother, who was Jamaican, at the age of two. His father, who spoke only Spanish, was forced into a soldiers' camp in Jamaica and then sent back to Cuba where Alphonso and his mother lost all contact with him. Alphonso went to boarding school at the Stony Hill Industrial School where he received his musical instruction, first on drums and then on saxophone, when his mother requested that he take up the saxophone instead. "I went to Stony Hill. There were two schools there that had the same position and I learned at Stony Hill. And furthermore, my mother was poor. She couldn't eat, she couldn't bring me up, so I was to go to school and I learned music, and I am happy about that today. I thank her for that and I thank the Lord for that. I started at the age of 10 and I never do no other work but music," Alphonso says. Alphonso left the school at age 17 and took a job performing for the Eric Dean Orchestra, a popular starting place for the Skatalites members. He left after only working there for a few months and performed for Redver Cooke's band at a hotel in Montego Bay. Alphonso performed with a number of other groups in the 1950s, and while performing for Baba

Motta's group, Alphonso met Lester Sterling in 1954. In 1956, Alphonso recorded for Coxsone, performing with Cluett Johnson (Clue J) and the Blues Blasters. Alphonso continued to record for Coxsone as a backing instrumentalist for many of his vocalists.

In the 1960s when ska began to emerge, instrumentalists like Alphonso were in huge demand. He therefore recorded for not only Coxsone, but other competitive producers, such as Duke Reid and Vincent "Randy" Chin. Even though Alphonso signed a contract to record exclusively for Coxsone, he broke it a week later in the land where money talks. Alphonso continued to perform for producers and labels, and even left Jamaica in 1963 to take an offer at the Cat & Fiddle Club in Nassau, Bahamas. A year later he had moved back and was a firm member of the Skatalites.

Cuban-born Roland Alphonso, tenor saxophonist for the Skatalites, at a performance in Chicago in 1997. Alphonso, an Alpha Boys School graduate, performed his entire life until he died after suffering a burst blood vessel onstage in 1998 (photograph Heather Augustyn).

"When the band started, when we were playing for Coxsone, McCook wasn't in Jamaica. He was in Nassau. So the band were Coxsone's musicians and make records for him and I have the records to prove it. Afterwards, we formed the band, Tommy come to the band, and the drummer and the bass player, Lloyds, they formed the band and they ask me to play with them and I play with them. And I play with them up to today which I am thankful to the Master for that because I'm just very thankful that the world know me and want to know me, and I'm very thankful for that," Alphonso says.

43

Alphonso and the rest of the Skatalites were the music behind the vocalists, the backing band, even providing the foundation for Bob Marley that very first time he hit the acetate on his debut song, "Simmer Down," which Doreen Shaffer still performs regularly as a tribute to her fellow musicians and a tribute to Marley and his family.

When the Skatalites went their separate ways in 1965, Alphonso found it easy to move on. In fact, even before the Skatalites performed for the last time in 1965, Alphonso had formed and performed with the Soul Brothers, a band that later became known as the Soul Vendors. He recorded for Bunny Lee, Leslie Kong, and more for Coxsone in subsequent years. "Coxsone is a producer and I record for him. Six days a week I make records for him. Up till now, I am a poor guy, babes. I'm a poor guy but I am happy because I learned to be comfortable and support my family," he says.

In 1969, Alphonso suffered a stroke and he and his family chose to emigrate to America where Alphonso played at a number of venues, including The Apache in Brooklyn. Here he was a mainstay, despite having limited dexterity in his right hand as a result of the stroke. In 1983, Alphonso reunited with the Skatalites at the Sunsplash Festival and then again in 1990 when he began touring and recording regularly with the group. "The band, we broke up in 1965. We started for one year and a couple months. But we started up again back up here and we stick together now. Our records spread all over the world," Alphonso says. He says he realizes they may not have been the ones who invented the style, but they were the ones who certainly

Skatalites tenor saxophone player Roland Alphonso (left) and alto saxophone player Lester Sterling perform at the University of Chicago in 1997 (photograph Heather Augustyn).

performed it. "Some of it started before me, but I am one of the men who get it popular because people love me. And when they hear me playin' ska, they say, 'Roland playing ska? Roland playing ska?' and they buy my record and I have fans all over the world today. Because when I go to Germany, I hear, 'Who's Alphonso? Who's Alphonso? You? How you so small?' (laughs)."

Roland Alphonso suffered a burst blood vessel in his head while performing onstage on November 2, 1998, at the Key Club on Sunset Boulevard in Hollywood. Fifteen days later he suffered another burst vessel and slipped into a coma. His family decided to remove him from life support and Alphonso died on November 20, 1998, at the age of 67.

Another member of the original Skatalites who became a frequent tourer in later decades was Skatalites drummer Lloyd Knibb. Born in Portland, Jamaica, in 1931, Knibb came to Kingston to attend school. "I didn't go to Alpha. I was self taught at my house. I teach myself," says Knibb. Upon graduation he performed in Montego Bay hotel bands as a drummer. His drumming character, a mix of calypso, Burru, and Rasta styles, came largely from the experience he gained from others, such as Count Ossie.

Count Ossie, whose real name was Oswald Williams, was a great friend to many jazz musicians in Jamaica in the 1940s and 1950s. He built a Rasta camp in East Kingston in the Wareika Hills where these jazz musicians could come and learn from each other and play together. It is Count Ossie's Burru style drumming, an African rhythm using three drums, that Prince Buster used on the very first recording he produced, "Oh, Carolina," by The Folkes Brothers. Duke Reid, in an attempt to squash Prince Buster's attempt to break into the recording business, bribed the studio booker at JBC Studios where Prince Buster was to record The Folkes Brothers and Count Ossie in this first foray into the business and took his time slot. Not to be deterred, Prince Buster went upstairs in the studio to utilize a tiny closet with a microphone set-up and knocked off the huge hit "Oh, Carolina," as well as two other songs, "Chubby" and "I Make a Man" after eight hours of frustrating toil. Although a hit in the dancehalls, "Oh, Carolina," like so many other ska hits, never received any radio play since ska was considered "ghetto music" and associated with the Rastafari who were ostracized by virtually every sector of Jamaican society. Count Ossie's was one place where Rastas and musicians could go to enhance their skills, share in spirituality, and enjoy camaraderie.

Knibb was one of the musicians who attended Ossie's Rasta camp so he was greatly influenced by the unique African rhythms he learned, as well as the jazz he listened to on the radio, by big band greats such as the Glen Miller Band. And Knibb himself played in these jazz bands while employed in the tourist hotels, working first for the Val Bennett Band, then the Stanley Headlam Band, the Jack Brown Band, and the Eric Dean Orchestra. "We used to play in a big band on Coney Island, a 12-piece, 14-piece band and we was all together in the same group all the time. We were a certain set of musicians, a certain set. We knew everything that happened and go from band to band, go from one group to the next, same set of band," he says. While in the Eric Dean Orchestra, Knibb had the chance to perform the popular jazz hits of the day, especially those from America, as well as Latin-infused rhythms, such as the bolero and cha-cha. Knibb utilized all of these experiences in his time with the Skatalites in the '60s, and after the Skatalites' last performance at the Runaway Bay Hotel for a police dance, Knibb performed for The Supersonics with Tommy McCook and then returned to the hotel circuit. He gathered with the Skatalites again in 1983 for the Sunsplash Festival and continues to tour with the Skatalites' current lineup. Knibbs says:

> I am the original drummer for the Skatalites. I was the original drummer for all recording sessions. Everyone, Duke Reid, Prince Buster, Coxsone, Treasure Isle, you name them all. I was the drummer they come to, for everybody. You name them all, Bob Marley, Ken Boothe, Derrick Morgan, Alton Ellis, everybody. Every show they go on are the same tunes we cut for them. I am the originator of the ska beat also. In the studio, me and Coxsone Downbeat try out a beat. My beat sound different, heavier, so my drumming is distinct. So most all the drummers try to play like me. They like the beat but then can't get it to sound like me. So that is how it started.

Upright bass player Lloyd Brevett is a sight, center stage with his long, thin dread locks and pork pie hat. Brevett began his schooling in music, not at the Alpha Boys School or other academic institution, but rather under the tutelage of his own father who was an accomplished professional musician himself. "My daddy, my daddy was a bass player," says Brevett. Brevett's father founded the Count Brevett Band in 1950 and taught his son to play bass, since he too was a bass player, as well as a saxophonist. The Count Brevett Band performed jazz, mento, calypso, and rhumba at Coney Island in Jamaica. There Brevett the senior played the upright bass while Brevett the junior helped to hold it, a true experiential learning of the instrument and music. Brevett also was taught by his father how to build his own upright bass by hand, furthering his intimate knowledge of the instrument.

Like many of the others, Brevett played in a variety of jazz bands in Jamaican hotels, such as the Eric Dean Orchestra, Lord Fly's band, and Sonny Bradshaw's orchestra (Bradshaw was a bandleader; organizer of the '83 Sunsplash Festivals and the festivals that followed in subsequent years; and host of his own traveling radio shows, *Teenage Dance Party* and *Jamaican Hit Parade*, much like a Jamaican version of Dick Clark). Brevett began to do studio work and met Tommy McCook and Don Drummond and then joined the Skatalites. "When we started, we never started in ska, we started in jazz. We were in separate bands in Jamaica. Big band, we started. I was 14 when I started to play in a big band. It was jazz and ballads. We started to play rhythm and blues, but jazz was still with it. We started to change the beat. We started to play ska, but we never really name it. But we play ska. Guitar, 'ska, ska, ska.' One guy come to the studio used to say, 'Wha'up, Skavoovie?' That guy was Cluet Johnson, bass player, joking guy. 'Wha'up, Skavoovie?' He came there so regular and talk Skavoovie, that together with the guitar, 'ska, ska, ska,' that name the music ska. Yeah. That is it," says Brevett. The term "Skavoovie" was also heard bantered around by Theophilus Beckford who played piano and is credited with the early Jamaican classic "Easy Snappin'," recorded by Coxsone in 1956 at Federal Studios. Beckford was killed at age 65 in February 2001, after he was wounded in the head by a hatchet in an altercation with an unidentified man in Kingston.

The Skatalites performed for all Jamaican vocalists of the time, says Brevett. "We play for all the record artist, all the artist. Jimmy Cliff, Prince Buster, Bob Marley. 'Simmer Down,' that's Bob Marley played by the Skatalites. All the artists then. Derrick Morgan. Any artist in

Jamaica at that time," says Brevett. Other artists who performed as studio musicians during this time include Oswald "Baba" Brooks, Rico Rodriguez, Val Bennett, Stanley "Ribs" Notice, and Arkland "Drumbago" Parks. But the members of the Skatalites got together to form their own union, for themselves, instead of for others. "Lloyd Brevett, Lloyd Knibb, Tommy McCook, Don Drummond, Roland Alphonso, Jah Jerry was the guitar, Ska Sterling, and carried on, carried on, and then Tommy McCook come out an join us in '62. In '62 Tommy McCook join us. At that time, we were young, in our 20s. Tommy McCook was the elder. Everyday we were making tunes. In 1962, he decided we need a little of the action," Brevett says.

Skatalites bassist Lloyd Brevett performs in Chicago in 1997. As a young child, Brevett learned bass from his father, founder of the Count Brevett Band. Brevett's walking-style bass lines and punctuated composition give the Skatalites' songs their classic energy (photograph Heather Augustyn).

After the band's breakup, Brevett performed with the Soul Brothers, the band that became the Soul Vendors. Brevett recorded his own solo album called *African Roots* that included some members of the Skatalites on it, and also featured Rasta music. Brevett joined the group at the Sunsplash Festival and toured with the reformation in the 1990s, but left again due to differences in style and discontent with the band being booked into smaller shows, he says. Shaffer says Brevett just needed to take time off for his health. "He wasn't keeping good health. Sometimes there's a little flare up so he was really ailing," says Shaffer.

Jackie Mittoo was the Skatalites' keyboardist and was born on March 3, 1948, in Browns Town in St. Ann's Parish in Jamaica. His birth name was Donat Roy Mittoo and at only age four he learned to play the piano from his grandmother. He first performed in public at age ten. Mittoo attended Kingston College and dropped out, but not before he met and performed with such greats as Augustus Pablo and Tyrone Downie of The Wailers, even teaching them. But Mittoo already had established a professional career, performing with bands like the Rivals and the Sheiks, when he met members of the Skatalites while performing in the studio. He continued to play for Coxsone at Studio One as one of his session musicians.

Even after his time with the Skatalites, Mittoo stayed on with Coxsone, performing with the Soul Brothers and then recording literally thousands of songs as a session musician for Coxsone through the '60s, '70s, and '80s. Even when Mittoo moved to Canada he still returned to work for Coxsone. After his Studio One days, Mittoo also performed for Bunny Lee and Sugar Minnott. In 1990, at only the age of 42, Mittoo died of cancer. His funeral was held at the National Arena in Jamaica and Coxsone attended, along with many others in the music industry who also performed.

The man most credited with playing that very first distinctive ska rhythm on his guitar was none other than the Skatalites' Jah Jerry, given the nickname because of his allegiance to Rastafarianism. He was born as Jerome Haynes, but some records indicate his last name was Hines or even Hinds, although he was no relation to the great vocalist Justin Hinds. Jah Jerry was born on August 11, 1921, and he grew up on the border of Trenchtown in Kingston in a section of the ghetto called Jones Town. Unlike many of the other members of the Skatalites, Jah Jerry didn't play an instrument during his childhood, even though his father, who was blind, did own a guitar.

Jah Jerry first began to learn the instrument in his 20s and, along with his father, Jah Jerry took guitar lessons from famous Jamaican guitarist Ernest Ranglin for many years. Jah Jerry then performed as a studio musician for Prince Buster on songs like The Folkes Brothers' "Oh,

Ska: An Oral History

Carolina" that Buster produced, and "They Got to Go," and for Leslie Kong with Derrick Morgan. It was while Jah Jerry performed for Prince Buster that he played the unique ska rhythm, according to Prince Buster. It was this distinctive style of guitar playing that not only defined ska, but became Jah Jerry's trademark of sorts. He played the chop, chop chords that gave ska songs their rhythm.

Jah Jerry performed with the Skatalites in the mid–60s and returned to studio work afterwards. He rejoined the Skatalites for the Sunsplash Festival in 1983 and performed on their 1984 album, *The Return of the Big Guns*, but left the band for good in 1985 to return to his hometown, Jones Town. He died at the age of 86, two days after his birthday, on August 13, 2007.

Johnny "Dizzy" Moore was the Skatalites' trumpeter, and as a child he wanted to be a musician so badly, he would even resort to trickery. Even though there was music in Moore's home, his parents discouraged him from playing. Moore says he would even roll up a pumpkin leaf into a little flute, or use a papaya stalk, just so he could play music because he loved it so much. He says he purposely created mischief so his parents would enroll him in the Alpha Boys School, which is exactly what they did. After Moore graduated from Alpha Boys School he gained employment, but not as a musician. He began his career as a typesetter for the *Jamaica Gleaner*, the leading newspaper on the island. He then joined the Jamaica military band to continue his love of music, but he was kicked out of the band after three and a half years for playing too much popular jazz. Moore began performing with dance bands around Jamaica, such as Stanley Edgar's band and Mapletoft Poulle's band, but left after he was asked to cut his hair and he refused. Moore was Rastafarian, and Rastafaris at that time in Jamaica were not accepted in conventional social circles, especially the high society that came to listen to the hotel bands. Rastafaris were brutalized by the police and oppressed by the government for their illegal use of ganja, their dreadlock hairstyles, and their misunderstood beliefs.

Moore went where many of his brethren went in the 1950s and 1960s, to Count Ossie's Rastafari camp in the Wareika Hills. There he performed regularly with his fellow Rasta musicians. But Moore soon found he needed to fulfill his urge to perform in public and left the camp in the hills to seek a performer's life that he could reconcile with his own lifestyle. Moore visited Coxsone and proposed that Coxsone record local artists to play on his sound system, rather than visiting America all of the time to buy R&B records. At first, Coxsone thought that Moore's idea was crazy and gave him the nickname "Dizzy" because of his plan, but soon Coxsone agreed. As Jamaican music segued into the studio, Moore became associated with the members of the Skatalites in the '60s, performing at dance halls and parties and finally living out his dream.

After the Skatalites split, Moore joined the Soul Vendors in England and then returned to Jamaica to perform with the Supersonics. In the new millennium, Moore and other Jamaican greats formed the Jamaica All Stars and toured the world. Music was Moore's life, and on October 16, 2007, Johnny "Dizzy" Moore was given the Order of Distinction in the rank of commander from the Jamaican Government "for pioneering work in popularizing Jamaican music." He died on August 16, 2008, after a long battle with colon cancer.

Shaffer's vocal partner was Jackie Opel, born Dalton Sinclair Bishop in 1938 in Bridgetown, Barbados. He came from a large family that was poor. He listened to radio stations broadcasting from Nashville and he grew to love the American rhythm and blues, which greatly influenced Opel's singing style. Opel began singing by swimming out to the tourist cruise ships that lined the Barbados coast, and he performed on stage at many of the Barbados hotels. Opel sang in his native country with an incredibly strong six-octave voice, which so impressed a visiting Byron Lee that Lee brought Opel to Jamaica to perform as the vocalist for the Dragonaires. But the relationship dissolved for unknown reasons after Opel and his Trinidadian wife arrived in Jamaica.

Opel became introduced to the members of the Skatalites and began singing for the musicians as well as in duets with Shaffer. Opel also arranged many of the Skatalites songs with Alphonso. One of Opel's most famous songs with Shaffer was the song, "The Vow." After the Skatalites broke up, Opel continued to perform for other Jamaican artists and was very prolific, performing with such greats as Bunny Wailer and Peter Tosh. Even though Opel was a popular Jamaican vocalist during these years, he moved to Trinidad and then back to his native Barbados where he continued to work and perform until he died in a car accident on March 8, 1970, in his hometown at the young age of 32.

When Doreen Shaffer joined together with the Skatalites, she was one of four vocalists the group used for their live performances. And because many of the Skatalites songs are instrumentals, the vocalists performed only a few tunes during each show. Still, in the short time the Skatalites were initially together and the small amount of stage time she received, Shaffer experienced a life that made her never want look back to the days of business school. Shaffer explains:

> I start with the band. I went to Studio One to do a recording for Coxsone Dodd. I had an appointment with Mr. Dodd. I was sent there by a friend. And then that day, they were supposed to record me, they said come back next week. He must have wanted them to do the recording. So I was doing some rehearsing in the studio and one of the band members, the drummer, Lloyd Knibb, said, "We'd love to have you in the band." However, I do the record and then I said yes. Jackie Opel and myself. Jackie Opel was a member of the band. He's now deceased. But at that time, when the band was formed, we had four vocalists at that time, I being the only female. You have Jackie Opel, Lord Tanamo, you have Tony DeCosta, he's also deceased, and myself. Then we started in shows and traveling all over the country.

After the Skatalites broke up in 1965, Shaffer continued singing, establishing herself further as an artist, but not without a snafu that had the potential to kill her budding career. Shaffer recalls:

> I started with the Skatalites in 1964 when the band formed and then we were off for a year and we got a job at the Bournemouth Beach Hotel in Jamaica [where the Skatalites had a residency] so I was there and I performed and someone was very interested in my performance and I was offered a job in the Bahamas. Unfortunately, that didn't come about. It should have been. You have these cruise ships that used to come there and they would dock. So I got a letter from them stating that they wanted me. I was supposed to attend an audition, which unfortunately, where I was living, I didn't really get nothing in the ghetto, the tenement, you know. Somebody took the letter and destroyed it. But I found out. They sent me another letter that they were waiting for me in Miami. So when I got the letter, all of this had gone. The date passed and I couldn't make it. They said they were waiting for me almost a

week, but like I said before, the letter was destroyed. They had got someone from Florida. Someone there got the opportunity I should have gotten.

But fortunately, Shaffer's talent was still in demand. "I went to the Bahamas finally. The people still were interested. They still make preparations for me. And I was there for like 18 months. I work at a club called The Island House and it was lovely. It was great. I wasn't too open and I didn't know what was going on around me, but I had a chaperone. I had someone there. Someone would always take me around and she get everything done, so I was half comfortable. That was good. I was in my late 20s, about 28," says Shaffer.

After Shaffer finished her work in the Bahamas, she returned to her native Jamaica and continued her career. "I came back to Jamaica and then I started recording. It was at the end of '79, I think, that I did, 'Sugar Sugar.' That was moving for me," she says. "Sugar Sugar" is a song that Shaffer regularly sings with the modern incarnation of the Skatalites and it was written for Shaffer by Laurel Aitken. Her other classics with the Skatalites include, "You're Wondering Now," and "Can't You See." "Most of the time, after the band broke up, I would do concerts around the island with a lot of other artists, some of them passed on. The New Caledonians, Delroy Wilson, the Itals, a few of them that I really worked with," she says.

In 1983, when the Sunsplash Festival took place, Shaffer was part of the Skatalites reunion. "I was still living in Jamaica and I think it was the Sunsplash organizers, they were the ones who got in touch with them [the members of the Skatalites] in some way and I was informed that they were going to come down for Sunsplash and they wanted me to be a part of it. But everybody was away. I hadn't seen them for a good while. So that was quite exciting, meeting everybody again. But I didn't get back with them until I got to the U.S., that's what I'm saying. Sunsplash was in '83, but they went on to London and I wasn't a part of that," says Shaffer.

Shaffer had a busy personal life and in the 1970s, before the reunion, she took time off from singing professionally to raise her family. "In my 20s, I was having kids. I have four kids. One is deceased, the eldest is abroad and no one sees, but two are here in the U.S. We don't live together. They are big people so they live on their own," she says from her home now in New York. She says she moved to the U.S. in 1992 after living in Jamaica her entire life. "My husband filed for the kids and me [through immigration]. And I came up in about '92. I had a tragic death. One of my kids died under tragic circumstances. This occurred in Jamaica. He came down and he said, 'Well, I can't do anything. I can't bring her back.' So we got married in June and she was buried down. We got married June ninth, she was buried on the sixth. It was in Kingston. It was a lot of ups and downs. You give up and you give in. But you have to go on. You can't give up. You have to take the good with the bad," she says.

When Shaffer arrived in the U.S., word of her presence quickly spread to the members of the Skatalites and Coxsone's wife facilitated the reunion. "Ms. Dodd took me down to Central Park. They were having some concert. They were part of this festival and she took me directly because she knew where to find them and she was the one who took me there. So I was happy, meetin' and greetin'. So we decided, they said, 'Well, you are here now, you've got to work with us,'" Shaffer says.

And she has toured with the Skatalites ever since then, traveling the country, traveling the globe. In 2008 alone, the Skatalites visited Brazil, France, England, the Netherlands, Luxembourg, Spain, Germany, Denmark, Sweden, Finland, Russia, the U.S., Canada, the Czech Republic, Poland, and Japan. "It's exciting. We have a lot of dates and a lot of audiences. It's very interesting. It's advanced, you know. Wherever we go, we have a full house, I would say. It's quite commending to know that after all these years, it pays off, all the time," Shaffer says.

Touring year after year with the members of the Skatalites has been a labor of love for Shaffer, even though being on the road and performing late at night in clubs is a difficult lifestyle for a grandmother in her 70s. "It's quite exhausting. We're doing shows and our nights are very hectic, so it's quite an experience, but I'm doing that and I thank god. I enjoy being on the road, but at the same time, you need your rest and you need to be with your family," she says. "But music is fun. If you enjoy it, it is worth it. A sacrifice. A lot of sacrifice. It's lot of devotion because it takes up a lot of your time," says Shaffer. And what do her grandkids think of grandma Shaffer? "Very awesome," she says with a sweet laugh.

Shaffer says she plans to keep bringing her music to fans all over the world. "I hope for the Skatalites everything good. Even better than last year, that everyone will be around and we put out more good music," she says, acknowledging that the music appeals to generations young and old, but the youth keep it alive. "The young ones, they go crazy. The kids, they are very excited and very into it, so I'm happy for that. The energy from the audience, that's what keeps me," Shaffer says.

The popularity of the Skatalites after all these years is a result of the work of the founders of the ska sound and those who formed the Skatalites, the true pioneers. The music they established led to modern versions of ska and other incarnations of the jazz and calypso blend. "You have a lot of dub music and hip hop going on, which is a part of the musical scene. Some people really want to hear instruments, to hear the band, the orchestra, and the music. These are great musicians, I have to give them credit, you know, because from Roland, Tommy, coming right down, Don Drummond, they were really good," she says.

CHAPTER THREE

Godfather of Ska: Laurel Aitken

IN JAMAICA, PRIOR TO THE 1950s, music had an important social function that contributed, not only to ska music, but specifically to the music of Laurel Aitken, Godfather of Ska. Aitken was a musician who performed for years before the ska explosion in Jamaica, due to his heritage as a Cuban, performing styles of music that were native to other islands, and derivatives of forms of music from Jamaica and the Caribbean. Although it is difficult to trace the musical ancestry in the Caribbean prior to the African slave trade of the 1600s, there is evidence to suggest that then, as well as after slave settlement, the music was dominated by drums, and therefore, rhythm.

As in America during the times of slavery, one of the only ways the slaves had for self expression and expression for the group was through music. When slaves in Jamaica enjoyed their drumming traditions of Africa, they were keeping a sense of their social identity. Music also served as a means of communication among slaves, such as when they blew a cow horn, called an abeng, they would secretly signal to each other to take up arms against the oppressor, a tradition strong in the lyrics of Jamaica's rebellion songs in future years.

But Jamaica was also inhabited by the Spanish and British, so it is not surprising that the African rhythms were influenced by the European styles of the colonizers. Therefore, Jamaican music in these times was a blend of these two worlds, a blend of black and white, two tones of music at the heart of Jamaican roots. And at its root too was the very reason for music in Jamaica — to serve a social function and bring comfort and hope in a traumatic time, binding people together.

Music on the Caribbean's other islands, such as Trinidad and Cuba, experienced a similar phenomenon due to the same social mix of African slaves and European oppressors. On Trinidad in the 1800s after emancipation, a Carnival celebration took place the two days prior to Ash Wednesday. This festival, called "Mas" by Trinidadians, which was short for masquerade, brought musicians out to the streets for music strong with rhythms played by sticks. Revelers marched through the streets in processions, carrying lit torches, a nod to the times of slavery when slaves assembled to put out the fires on the plantations. Sometimes these groups engaged in the custom of stick fighting, a display of power and skill that involved boastful threats and challenges, not unlike the musical wars of Prince Buster and Derrick Morgan, and those that followed. But when stick fights were banned by the white government in the 1890s, festival musicians used other instruments of rhythm, rather than sticks. They used whatever was available to them, such as spoons, pans, bottles, and even garbage can lids. The Trinidad steel pan band was born.

From these instruments emerged the Trinidad musical form of calypso. This genre was rooted in the call and response format of African slave music, and the call and response foundation of the Carnival stick fights. The lyrics of Trinidad calypsos were frequently full of these mock, playful challenges to a competitor. And the call and response pattern also engaged the community. It was an interactive musical form that bound together those who sang and played with those that heard. Jamaica had a calypso form all its own. This musical genre was called mento and it was not as aggressive lyrically, or cheeky, but it had its own local flavor.

Mix this together with an artist of Cuban descent and the product is uniquely Laurel Aitken, Godfather of Ska. "I've been singing since I was a little boy. Eight or ten," says Aitken, who was born in Cuba in 1927. "My language is Spanish because I am a Cuban and I went to Jamaica when I was eleven years old. My dad was a Jamaican, my mother was a Cuban, and he just wanted to go home and build his way in Jamaica. And ever since, I've been singing. I sing in different languages, such as Spanish, Italian, and French, and a bit of English," he says. His younger brother, Bobby Aitken, was also a popular Jamaican musician.

Aitken says that he listened to and learned the musical forms of the island as well as the music of America, which led to his own style. "I've been singing lots of different types of music before ska, such as calypsos, which was Jamaica's and Trinidad's music. But in the '50s and '60s, we used to dance to American music, New Orleans music, rhythm and blues. Rosco Gordon, Smiley Lewis, Big Joe Turner, and Louis Jordan. If you listen to early ska, it's boogie-woogie, rhythm and blues. That's where ska actually came from. We mixed the boogie-woogie style with calypso music. And that became ska. You mix calypso and rhythm and blues and just play the guitar, just shuffle the guitar like the American does with rhythm and blues, but the rhythm and blues forty years ago. You know that shufflin' guitar? Well that's ska," Aitken says.

He says the way that ska music started in Jamaica was organic and a product of all of the conditions present, rather than one person's creation. "No one anybody started doing that, but it was a good flavor. It flavored the songs the way people were dancing in those days, so in a way, ska just came, you get what I mean? Boogie-woogie — that's what we used to call ska in 1957, 1958, 1959, '60 until they start using lots of brass. You get what I mean? And they make it a bit more jazzy. There's no direct person that really said, 'Well this is ska.' We use the American shuffle on the guitar and put it with calypso, mixed with American music, and that was ska," says Aitken.

Godfather of ska Laurel Aitken performs in Chicago in 1997. The Cuban-born ska singer who died in 2005, blended boogie-woogie tunes with ska to create a skinhead legacy (photograph Heather Augustyn).

Aitken took his special blend

to the stage, working on cruise ships in Kingston Harbor as a teenager. When Aitken was only 15 years old, he won the *Vere Johns Opportunity Hour.* Aitken then turned to making money and after numerous successful wins at the talent show, he was very marketable in the tourist trades. "I used to play for the Jamaican Tourist Board. I used to sing and welcome the tourists coming from other countries in a big hut—you know, the calypso huts? And pretty loud colored shirts and sing them 'Welcome to Jamaica.' That's what I used to do. Then I used to sing at night at a club called the Colony Club and I used to sing calypso there, so I am coming from the roots of Jamaican music," says Aitken. But his career reached the point of no return when he met Chris Blackwell.

Chris Blackwell was born in 1937 in London. His father was Irish and his mother was Costa Rican and they were very wealthy. When Blackwell was young, they moved to Jamaica since his mother had family on the island. When Blackwell was 21 years old, he had an experience that converted him, changing the path of his life. One day, Blackwell was stranded, alone, on a reef. The hot Jamaican sun dehydrated Blackwell and his skin burned terribly as he fell into unconsciousness. A group of Rasta fisherman discovered Blackwell and rescued him, restoring him to health. This event occurred at a time when Rastas and their dreadlocks were not socially accepted by many people, especially the white elite. But Blackwell had been saved by the kindness of the men and he promised to champion their culture in the world. The way he chose to present Jamaican culture to the world was through their music, and Blackwell became one of the biggest music producers in history.

Blackwell invested $1,000 to begin his own music label, Island Records, and produced his first Jamaican recording which instantly became a number one hit on the island. The artist he recorded was none other than Laurel Aitken.

> I was the first man to make a Jamaican hit on the *Hit Parade* in Jamaica. I did that for Mr. Chris Blackwell, which afterward he became Bob Marley's manager. Island Records was the name of the company. In those days we didn't have any of our music in the chart until 1958. The chart just had American music. And then we made our own chart, the Jamaican chart, and it was called *Teenage Dance Party.* And the record I did for Mr. Chris Blackwell on Island Records in 1958, that was the very

first, a double A side, "Boogie In My Bones" on one side and the other side was "Little Sheila" which was the A side, and that was eleven weeks number one. It was eleven weeks number one in Jamaica. And it was a very big hit over there, and after that, everyone start making Jamaican music.

Chris Blackwell eventually left Jamaica after he signed such huge artists as Bob Marley, Toots and the Maytals, Burning Spear, Sly & Robbie, Third World, and Black Uhuru to the Island label. He left to return to the land of his birth, England, where he signed U2, Tom Waits, Cat Stevens, and PJ Harvey, among other legendary musicians and bands. And like Blackwell, Aitken too left Jamaica for England, for the second chapter of his career — a chapter no less successful than the first. Aitken says:

I was so famous in Jamaica and I was making money but wasn't able to live the way I thought I should be living. I moved to England in 1960. When I came to England there were about three of my records that had been pirated. 'Boogie In My Bones/Little Sheila' was pirated and two other songs were pirated. People just put them out, which they didn't have any right to do. And then I went to the only reggae/ska company in England and I signed a contract, which was a bad contract, you know what I mean? It didn't make me happy at all because in Jamaica in those days you didn't use a contract, you just make records. And that was the first company I decided to make record with and they gave me a bad contract. Melodisc Records. Some people call it Blue Beat Records.

The reason Aitken contends that those two names are sometimes interchangeable is because of the pirating scheme that Aitken had uncovered. Melodisc, Aitken discovered, was the label that had been pirating his songs. Emil Shalit was the owner of this label and responsible for the crime. But the solution wasn't as easy as crying foul that Shalit had profited at the expense of Aitken. Shalit had also done much more. He had made Aitken a star in England, leading to his international fame. Catching a whiff of this money, Aitken decided to strike up a deal with Shalit. They created the Blue Beat label, an imprint of Melodisc, dedicated to recording Jamaican music. He recorded the songs "Tough Man Tough" and "Telephone" with backing from Georgie Fame & The Blue Flames, a white act that performed rhythm and blues and jazz and later recorded the song "Do the Dog" that became the inspiration for the Specials' famous track of the same name. But Aitken says the deal with Shalit was not a good one.

"The name Blue Beat originated in England and I was the first Jamaican artist during that era that was signed to Melodisc Records to make that kind of music. I made quite a lot of records on that label because I would sign up with them for four years and I decided to take them to court about the contract and I couldn't get out of the contract. I had to do the four years. Then I signed up with a big company called EMI. I was with EMI for a little while and after living here a while I recorded for a lot of small companies and I also put out my own records as well," he says.

One of those companies that Aitken recorded for was Palmer Records, a label in England that also released Derrick Morgan's material. The label was known more commonly as Pama Records. And for Aitken, Pama Records was quite literally a financial gift, but also provided another contract with a caveat. After playing a show in Birmingham, England, in 1960, Aitken was arrested and taken to jail for non-payment of child support. The fine was 200 British pounds or else Aitken would have to serve six weeks in prison. So Aitken reached out to someone he knew would help because he had something of value — his talent and marketability. He called the owner of Pama Records, who paid Aitken's fine in return for a signed contract to record, and Aitken willingly signed, albeit with his back up against the wall. Aitken recorded for Pama Records in 1969 and 1970, recording such songs as "Landlords and Tenants," "Scandal in a Brixton Market," "Pussy Price," "Woppi King," "Skinhead Train," "Fire In Mi Wire," "Rise & Fall," and "It's Too Late," which were popular with the newly emerged skinhead culture.

The skinhead culture in England arose out of the more aggressive mod culture of the mid–'60s, and in response to the hippie culture and populations of preppy students that flourished in the preceding years. So in 1969, the skinhead culture emerged, perhaps first in the East End of London. Dress was characterized by rolled-up jeans, combat boots, thin braces (called suspenders in the U.S.), and a Ben Sherman shirt, or a similar button-down style. Hair was either completely shaven or worn short. Girls wore mini skirts, tights, combat boots or oxfords or loafers, and a permanent press shirt, with or without braces. Hair styles worn by girl skins, or lady birds, were short on top and fringed and long around the edges, varying in length.

Skinhead dress may have been a response to styles that surrounded the era, but there is also evidence to suggest that some of the dress code may have come as a transition from the rude boy look in Jamaica. In Jamaica, clothing and a sharp look were important to rude boys who wanted to attract attention. They wore suits made of shiny fabric that glistened in the night club lights, and a pork pie hat was common. This hat featured a narrow brim and Laurel Aitken was almost never without one on.

Dress code was important as a group distinction, and styles segued from Jamaica into the wardrobes of white culture in England, especially in the working class. And Desmond Dekker himself may be responsible for one characteristic of skinhead dress in particular. When Desmond Dekker came to the U.K. in 1967, he was given a stylish suit by his recording company, Creole. He cut six inches off the bottoms of the suit pants to don a new style. All of the kids responded to this style by rolling up the bottoms of their pants, a style that became part of the skinhead dress code.

But the connection between skinhead and Jamaican cultures was more than just the clothing — it was the music. West Indian music played in bars in North Kent, Sheffield, Bristol, Birmingham, and Brixton. These bars were frequented by white kids, therefore the cultures mixed. Aitken played at many of these locations and was a favorite of skins. And the love was returned. Aitken professes a love for skinheads who have supported him for decades, and he even proclaims himself the Boss Skinhead in his song he wrote for his fans and friends, "Skinhead Train." Aitken speaks before the song kicks in:

> This is your Boss Skinhead speaking
> On the skinhead train to Rainbow City.
> Sit back, relax
> Have a Coke, crack a joke,
> Put on your dancing shoes
> And listen while your Boss Skinhead
> Sock it to you.

In another of Aitken's skinhead-themed songs, plainly titled "Skinhead," he recognizes the sharp look of his fellow skins.

> When a skinhead
> Walks down the street
> Every chick heart
> Skip a beat.

The rude boy and rude boy culture were also important to Aitken's song content and he recorded tunes in their honor, such as "Rudy Got Married," which made the U.K. charts in 1981. Rude boys and skinheads so loved Aitken they gave him his nickname, Godfather of Ska. "I was playing at a big ska club in London and the emcee, when it was my time to play, just came out and said, 'And now we bring to you, the Godfather of Ska, Laurel Aitken and the Pressure Tenants,' which is the name of one of my records, 'The Landlords and Tenants.' The band was called Pressure Tenants," says Aitken.

In the years that followed, Laurel Aitken toured and recorded periodically until his death from a heart attack in Leicester on July 17, 2005, at the age of 78. He performed only months before his death with amazing passion and energy, fueled by his fans, always singing his favorite song at every show, "Sally Brown." And although doctors told him in his later years not to dance, he still performed one hundred percent. He sang in other languages to spread his music all over the world and his fans were bound together by Aitken's charisma and spirit.

But it was a tough life. Aitken left Jamaica to seek the attention he thought he deserved, and England's music scene ebbed and flowed for Aitken. The music business was filled with false promises many times for Aitken. The *Jamaica Gleaner* ran an article the day after his death that revealed he was "bitter" over not receiving a national honor for his contribution to Jamaican culture. When Aitken is remembered, it is for his connection to his fans and his love for them that he shared through his music, for the rudies, the skinheads, and the fans in countries all over the world he sang to in their native tongues. "I'm very happy, in many ways," Aitken said.

CHAPTER FOUR

Passion and Revival: Toots Hibbert

EVEN IN THE VERY EARLY DAYS of life, music for Toots Hibbert was a passion, a spiritual experience, an expression of inside emotion toward the outside existence of man. Born Frederick Hibbert in 1945, in May Pen, in the parish (a Jamaican state) of Clarendon, Jamaica, Hibbert was the baby of the family, one of seven children.

Music was a crucial part of this deeply religious family. They attended services by the Seventh Day Adventist denomination in addition to others. "When I was growing up, before I start singing, I was going to school and going to church. I'd go to government school, then I'd go to church. They sing in the church all the time. That was my kind of music — church. I grew up listening to people who can sing, like from the other churches as well as listening to the radio," says Hibbert. In the 1950s and 1960s, the radio stations Jamaicans listened to were broadcast from New Orleans, and even the local stations in Jamaica played American rhythm and blues. "I listened to Mahalia Jackson, Elvis Presley, Ray Charles, James Brown, a lot of great people. And I listened to them over the radio. Yeah, mon, so that's how I come to love singing," Hibbert says.

When Hibbert was only 13 years old, still a student in school, he left his home in the countryside to explore life in Kingston. Like Prince Buster, Hibbert was a boxer in his youth, but he left that activity to try a different calling. "When I leave my country, I'm from the countryside, the countryside of Jamaica, May Pen. I was born down there, then I came to Kingston looking for my bigger brother, a place called Trenchtown where all the great music people live, in Trenchtown in Kingston. So I go and look for my brother sometimes and go back to country and the next holiday came back to Kingston again in Trenchtown and visited and I meet people. I meet Jimmy Cliff and I met Bob Marley and I met other great people. They told me one day I am going to be great because they like my voice," Hibbert says. But he didn't immediately enter the world of music and instead ended up in another field entirely. "Before I start my career, I used to do barbering. I used to be a barber and I cut hair. I learned to cut people's hair and while I do that I get me a little small guitar, like a mandolin guitar, and I learned myself to play that. When I'm not cutting hair, I play that and I get to learn from other musicians," he says.

Hibbert wanted to pursue a singing career and tried to get work with Leslie Kong, but was initially rejected. Derrick Morgan, who worked for Leslie Kong, remembers, "I didn't start Toots because Toots came to me and I turned him down because I do auditions for Beverly's (Kong)." But then Hibbert met Nathaniel "Jerry" Matthias and Ralphus "Raleigh" Gordon in 1964 and formed a singing group backed by the Skatalites, recording at Studio One for Coxsone. The sound of the early Maytals, who were later called The Flames by Island Records in England, was heavily influenced by Hibbert's gospel roots. They frequently performed with such backup bands as The Vikings or The Royals. The first album released by Studio One was entitled *Hallelujah* and combined Hibbert's gospel style with ska. This blend was an immediate success. "When I start singing in 1964 I did a lot of number one records. I did a song called, "It's You," and "Daddy." Both songs, one called "It's You," and the flip side called "Daddy," and I got number one record, two sides hit, two sides number one. I was the only singer in Jamaica that ever did that," says Hibbert. Hibbert not only sang with the Maytals, but he also sang with a duo called Bunny and Skitter in a song named "Get Ready."

The Maytals stayed with Studio One for two years and then recorded for Prince Buster, making hit songs such as "Broadway Jungle" and "Judgment Day." Hibbert says he left Coxsone for Prince Buster because he felt he could make more money with Prince Buster, but he found that Prince Buster didn't pay him well either. So in 1965, Hibbert and the Maytals left Prince Buster to record for Byron Lee, and in 1966 they won Jamaica's Festival Song Contest with the song "Bam Bam" that

Lee produced. Byron Lee and the Dragonaires were the backing band for this song. It seemed that success was eminent for the Maytals, until their rise was derailed when Hibbert was arrested on a marijuana possession charge and sent to prison.

Hibbert contends that he was not jailed for ganja and instead was the object of ill will. Traditional Jamaicans, especially those in rural areas, such as the countryside in which Hibbert was raised, believed that bad luck could befall someone when evil conspired against that person. Hibbert says that he was set up and he was framed because some people were jealous at his career success. He says at that time in his life he had never even smoked ganja and he wrote about his experience in his hit song, "54-46 Was My Number."

> Stick it up mister!
> Hear what I say sir!
> Get your hands in the air sir!
> And you will get no hurt mister no, no, no.
> I said yeah, listen what I say.
> Don't you hear I said yeah, listen what I say.
> Do you believe I would take something with me
> and give it to the policeman?
> I wouldn't do that.
> And if I'd do that, I would say sir,
> "Go on and put the charge on me."
> I wouldn't do that.
> I'm not a fool to hurt myself,
> so I was innocent of what they done to me.
> They was wrong.
> Give it to me one time.
> Give it to me two times.
> Give it to me three times.
> Give it to me four times.
> 54-46 was my number.
> Right now someone else has that number.

Hibbert admits he made up the number "54-46" for the song and that wasn't actually the number assigned to him in prison, but the experience was real, and Hibbert spent 18 months in jail. To the great benefit of both Hibbert and the Maytals, the Maytals decided to wait for Hibbert to be released from jail instead of finding another lead man.

But then Hibbert and the Maytals had to find another producer, since Byron Lee wasn't as loyal or patient, and Hibbert returned to the man that once told him no — Leslie Kong. Kong recognized the Maytals' success prior to Hibbert's imprisonment, seeing his popularity with the people and the potential for more hits, and so Kong produced "54-46" which became an immediate sensation. In 1969, Toots and the Maytals recorded a song that was a playful jab at Kong, since they now had a professional and lucrative relationship, but Hibbert still smarted from

Frederick Hibbert, better known as Toots of Toots and the Maytals. Hibbert learned to sing as a child while attending the Seventh Day Adventist Church in May Pen, Clarendon, Jamaica, where his family were members. As a result, his songs always have a deeply spiritual feel (photograph courtesy Mike Cacia).

his earlier snub. The song "Monkey Man" was a huge hit and today has been covered by dozens of bands and featured in American commercials and even children's cartoons like *The Wild Thornberrys*.

The monkey in Jamaican folklore is a common character that stems from African tradition, along with the Anansi, frequently a spider or insect, and the tiger. The monkey in Jamaican culture symbolizes the white man and Hibbert is one of many Jamaican artists to sing of this character. Others include Justin Hinds & the Dominoes who recorded "The Higher the Monkey Climbs" in 1966, produced by Duke Reid, a revealing commentary on the unethical nature of white man's success; and Derrick Harriott's "Monkey Ska." "Monkey Man" became the first international hit for Toots & the Maytals, charting in the U.K. in 1970.

Another influential song of this era was the Toots & the Maytals tune "Do the Reggay," recorded in 1968. This was the first song to use the word reggae in a title, even though the spelling was different than the spelling now used. Hibbert explains,

> I carry on and carry on and carry on until reggae start to play and then invent the word reggae. Reggae was played and no one know what to call it. I think it was in the '60s and people always called it "boogie beat" and "blue beat," and it was kind of a crazy beat that people loved but you know, white people came down from England, from America, Hawaii, all over the world and when they came to Jamaica they enjoy Jamaican music but they didn't know what the music called, until one day, I sit down, me and my two friends that used to sing together, I say, let's make some song and that word just come out my mouth. Do the reggay, you know? And we think it's a joke until people take it very serious. I named the record, the style of music, called "Do the Reggay." That's why it's good to be Jamaican. Because I'm Jamaican I can do all these things and a lot of people can come and enjoy, so I'm the inventor for the word reggae.

But other musicians disagree with Hibbert and claim that reggae was named after the Jamaican slang term for a prostitute, a "streggae," and when radio stations in Jamaica refused to play this style of music because of the suggestive name, the name was modified to "reggae." But Hibbert's song was, undeniably, the first to use the word reggae in the title, no matter the spelling.

Lester Sterling of the Skatalites contends he was the one who first created the genre of reggae in the same year Hibbert released his song. It was a fruitful time with synergy and crossover between artists and studios. "Reggae actually start in 1968. First reggae song ever made, I did it, named 'Bang-a-rang.' That was a number one hit. A big hit. That's when reggae started," says Sterling.

Hibbert doesn't claim to be the inventor of reggae though, only the inventor of the word. And in fact, he has profound respect for those who came before him and helped to establish the environment that made his success possible. "When I came to Kingston, they [Bob Marley and Jimmy Cliff] were a little bigger than me. They were singing before me and start before me. They were older than me. I get to meet them and I like them and they like me and afterward we love each other, you know? It was a good thing to meet Bob Marley, meet Jimmy Cliff, meet Alton Ellis, good people. I meet them before my career even started, so it was pretty cool, you know?" he says.

Hibbert and Cliff came together again when they both worked on the film *The Harder They Come*, the classic Jamaican movie staring Jimmy Cliff as Ivanhoe Martin, a young musician at first exploited by the corrupt music industry, then turned wise but beyond redemption. The movie was based on the real-life boy-turned-bad of the same name, Ivanhoe Martin, who went by the nickname Rhyging, a Jamaican patois for "angry" and "wild." Rhyging was a hero and legend to those in the ghetto since he outsmarted the authorities for so long in 1948, much like a John Dillinger or Bonnie and Clyde. He wore two side pistols and engaged in several shootouts with the law. The *Jamaica Gleaner* labeled Rhyging "Jamaica's most resourceful violent criminal" and questioned, "In the aftermath of the grim finale, the question on everybody's lips was, who was Rhyging, this little man who had mocked the efforts of the entire police establishment for so long and who had either coerced or inspired so much loyalty from his friends?" Rhyging was the original rude boy and his story is truly the stuff of movies.

Hibbert's song "Pressure Drop" was featured on the movie soundtrack, and both the soundtrack and many of the singles became huge hits. The song "Many Rivers to Cross" by Jimmy Cliff chronicled Cliff's character's demise, as well as the social conditions in Jamaica during the late '60s and early '70s:

Many rivers to cross
But I can't seem to find my way over
Wandering I am lost
As I travel along the white cliffs of Dover
Many rivers to cross
And it's only my will that keeps me alive
I've been licked, washed up for years
And I merely survive because of my pride
And this loneliness won't leave me alone
It's such a drag to be on your own
My woman left me and she didn't say why
Well, I guess I'll have to cry
Many rivers to cross
But just where to begin I'm playing for time
There have been times I find myself
Thinking of committing some dreadful crime
Yes, I've got many rivers to cross
But I can't seem to find my way over
Wandering, I am lost
As I travel along the white cliffs of Dover
Yes, I've got many rivers to cross
And I merely survive because of my will...

Hibbert's song "Pressure Drop," in the film, captured the mood and build-up to the movie's final tragic ending. Hibbert was skillful in anthologizing the difficult times in Jamaica. He gave validation to the struggles faced by everyman. He brought recognition to the problems suffered by the people of his country — poverty, unemployment, homelessness. "I was singing about hard times. When you go through hard times like my people have been through, you got to write about it, write a song about it. Don't make it sound like politics. It's not politics. Just sing about real things that can affect you and can happen to a lot of people too. You don't have to be real, but it's real things that we sing about," says Hibbert. "It was tough. You couldn't get through. You couldn't get through to do what you wanted to do, but it was better than now because now, well in those days people don't kill people like that. But now people just kill people because of drugs, no good conscience, no good love to each other," Hibbert says.

Woven into "Time Tough" and his acknowledgment and validation of the social condition is an affirmation for the listener, an emotional appeal, an "Amen." And that "Amen" was also a critical component of Hibbert's music, drawn from his days singing in church. Beyond Hibbert's gospel sounds are his words that journal the difficult times and offer hope, in the song "Time Tough" through prayer, and in the 1972 Jamaican Festival Song Contest winner "Pomps and Pride," through one's own spirit. And certainly songs like "The Sixth and Seventh Books," "Hallelujah," "Matthew Mark," "Heaven Declare," "He'll Provide," "Judgment Day," and "Thy Kingdom Come" are entirely founded upon Hibbert's religious upbringing. His music truly brought gospel, through both its sound and its content, together with ska and reggae.

In the time since those early incubator years in Jamaica, Hibbert's music has only grown in popularity while other musicians have become part of the past. Hibbert was able to maintain his stature in the music world by conferring more than just his talent for music, but by also adapting his skill to the wants and needs of his loyal audiences.

In the late 1970s, when ska and reggae music experienced a revival in England, Toots & The Maytals felt that revival too. 2Tone bands such as the Specials covered Hibbert's song "Monkey Man" with a punky reggae spirit, and the Selecter covered "Pressure Drop." Hibbert's original songs had more than a new sound, they also had a new audience, the British youth, who were hungry for their music and had reverence for the original artists.

Hibbert's music also sustained because of the crossover appeal to other audiences. Fans of gospel, soul, rhythm and blues, and funk identified with Hibbert's special blend of these forms with ska and reggae. This musical depth kept audiences engaged in Hibbert's music across the decades. Hibbert also covered other musicians' songs, further extending his reach into additional genres and additional audiences. Hibbert covered "Louie Louie" by the Kingsmen with a funky James Brown-style, and he covered "Take Me Home, Country Roads" by John Denver with a smooth reggae rhythm.

Partnerships with other more mainstream artists also helped Hibbert to have continued career success. "I toured with the Rolling Stones. I toured with Buddy Guy. I toured with a lot of really great people," says Hibbert, who still tours four times a year and lives in Jamaica with his wife. They have seven children.

Hibbert even collaborated with other musicians for his 2004 release *True Love*, which won a Reggae Grammy. This album featured many of Hibbert's classic hits re-recorded with musicians such as Bonnie Raitt, Shaggy, No Doubt, Marcia Griffiths, Bunny Wailer, and Willie Nelson.

Needless to say, the music of Toots Hibbert influenced many listeners as well as many musicians and brought to the people the promise of revival. Dave Wakeling of the English Beat says of Hibbert, "He's a perfect example of how you can sing in an uplifting beat about situations of social deprivation. And I think that's what we've learned from that. Although life is tragic, it's still beautiful, and that if you contemplate on that part of it, the tragedy doesn't disappear, but it becomes easier to bear."

CHAPTER FIVE

Big Man: Judge Dread

ALEXANDER MINTO HUGHES, the artist better known as Judge Dread, named after the character in the famous Prince Buster and Derrick Morgan clash, was a big man. Physically, he was a presence on the stage, large but gentle. But more than a big, fat, nearly bald (except for a fringe of long locks on the back of his head) white man, Judge Dread was a big man in character and spirit. Like a musical Benny Hill, Judge Dread was bawdy, naughty, and liked to sing about, ahem, himself and his prowess. And it was in both of these ways, both physically and creatively, that Judge Dread became a legend.

Alex Hughes, born on May 2, 1945, grew up in Brixton in England. Here he lived among the immigrants from Jamaica who naturally came to England as a result of the open migration during days of colonization prior to independence. "I was born in a black area of Brixton. I came from Brixton where the first West Indians arrived just after the war and they actually arrived in that area, because they were some Jamaican pilots in the war. As a special thank you, the British government, 500 of them, come over with their families and billeted them in the air raid show just down the road from Brixton and that's how they actually started in Brixton with the first black kids, the first wave of Jamaican immigrants, and I sort of grew up with the music," he says.

Not only did Hughes grow up with the music, buying records right off the planters, or banana boats from the islands as they came into the port, but he also lived with the artists themselves. They were all neigh-

73

bors in Brixton. "When we're talking Jamaican music, for instance, Laurel Aitken, I've known since I was 14. Laurel used to live no more than three streets away from me. With Laurel, when I was 17 or 18 years old, I go into where Laurel was recording or meet Laurel in the illegal Jamaican clubs. Derrick Morgan is exactly the same. Derrick is a very old friend of mine, just like Laurel. With Marley, I've known Marley since 1960-something. I've got photographs of Marley way at the gap service station where the bands used to stop all those years ago. And everybody, like Desmond Dekker, I picked Desmond up from the airport in 1969. He had never met an Englishman before. And the Pioneers the same," he says. Many Jamaicans tried their hand in England where their music had appeal with the West Indian immigrants and blue collar youth, either traveling to perform for a few months at a time, or relocating altogether. Some sound system operators, like Duke Vin and Count Suckle, became music promoters for Jamaican music in England where they found crowds that welcomed them warmly. Hughes too found this crowd supportive, and so he in turn supported it back.

One way Hughes supported Jamaican music was by helping to launch the career of Bob Marley, he says.

> I was one of the instigators of starting Marley's image off. I used to write for a music paper called *The Record Mirror* which was really famous. I was actually the journalist for them and I remember Chris Blackwell calling me up saying, "Look, I've spent so much money on Marley and he hasn't really happened. We're going to go bust if we don't do something about it," so I started writing up these articles on this Rasta man and the music stations, the radio stations, bit into it because in them days, if you said something in the *Record Mirror*, it had to be true. It was the Bible. It's like being on the cover of *Rolling Stone*. If you're on the cover of *Rolling Stone*, you're made, or *Vogue*, or anything like that. That's it. In them days, the *Record Mirror* would say, "Yes, this is going to be the greatest thing in the world," and then they start saying what you've been saying. They start repeating it over the radio. "Yes, this guy is so talented and he's an Ethiopian," and things like that, bearing in mind Bob Marley was part white. You tell people enough, they'll believe it.

Hughes was practically family with the ska musicians who came to live or record in England, growing up with them. And in 1963, when

Hughes became a bouncer at a club popular with the mod culture in Brixton called the Ram Jam Club, Hughes entered the world of entertainment. It was at this time that Hughes met Prince Buster. "In 1963, I started work in a club in Brixton as a door man, a bouncer, as they say, and of course, Prince Buster came up there then," he says. Other famous musicians, such as Tina Turner and Rod Stewart came to the club, and Hughes even let Stewart in to sing before he became famous. Because of Hughes's strength and size, he was even hired and worked as a security guard for the Rolling Stones. But Hughes's love was Jamaican music, so he saved his money and bought the equipment to launch his own career.

"I started my own mobile DJ and the words

Alex Hughes, better known as Judge Dread, grew up in Brixton with Jamaican immigrants and claims to have started white reggae, or what he calls "Dread Rock." Beloved by skinheads and music fans the world over, Hughes died of a heart attack in 1998, while performing on stage (photograph courtesy Alex Hughes).

Judge Dread have always been made up of a mythical judge in Jamaica that gave everyone sort of really strange sentences of 400 years and that sort of thing. And so what happened is, I called the name of my sort of sound system, I was a white man playing a black sound system, I actually called it Judge Dread's Sound Machine and what happened, in obviously the later years, I became basically a debt collector for Trojan Records. That's when I started to use the name more professionally," says Judge Dread.

Judge Dread then made the rather easy transition to performing by playing the instrumental or dub B-sides of the record singles and toasting his own lyrics against the instrumentals, a skill he learned from the Jamaican masters. "It evolved from playing the records and toasting over the top of the records, to when I finally went into the studio, which was basically in the '70s. I went in there and I made me first record," he says. Judge Dread's fans requested his toasting over an Ernest Ranglin song so often that Judge Dread grew tired of performing it. So he went into the studio to record a version of it he could play, rather than perform. When he played it one day at Trojan Records where he was employed, it caught the attention of the owner, and even though the company produced some forty records a week through the main label and its imprints, the owner liked the song so much, he began recording Judge Dread, who definitely had his own creative flair.

"I crossed over from recording on sort of a black label, my first quarter of a million records I ever sold were actually sold to the West Indians, because they all thought I was black," he says. The first song Judge Dread recorded was "Little Boy Blue," also known as "Big 6," after the popularity of Prince Buster's hit, "Big 5." The owner of Trojan Records that Judge Dread talks of was Lee Gopthal. This song reached #11 in 1972 on the U.K. Singles Chart, only the beginning of quantifiable success for Judge Dread. He followed this initial success with other "Big" hits, such as "Big 7," which charted #8, and "Big 8," which charted #14. These were also naughty nursery rhymes that were popular for their talent and audacity. Although Hughes was innovative, creating his own bawdy version of nursery rhymes, he was not new to using nursery rhymes in ska songs. Jamaican artists in the '60s also popularized nursery rhymes, most notably Eric "Monty" Morris with his songs "Humpty Dumpty," "Solomon Grundy," and the duet with Roy Panton titled "In and Out the Window." The "Big" series made Judge Dread a big star. "All of a sudden one of the major labels took a distribution deal because they realized that I was white and the next thing you know, I began to sell in the millions. In 1974, I was the biggest selling singles artist in Great Britain and during that time, I was selling an average of something like 78,000 a day," he says.

Like the PMRC (Parents' Music Resource Center) in the U.S. in the '80s was a group intent on censoring creativity in the name of their own agenda, so too were forces at work in the U.K. And Judge Dread with his saucy lyrics was a prime target. But the impact was exactly what Judge Dread wanted — an increase in his popularity. "I became a pop star because a lady named Mary Whitehouse in our country, she's the head of the anti-porn, anti-whatever, you know, you name it, the woman said something about it, but all she's really doing is building her own nest. But of course, the greatest thing she's done with me, because I made up nursery rhymes, she then said that I was corrupting the minds of the children, and of course that was the worst thing she could've ever done because that was it. I was having two records in the top 20 a week and neither one was being played on our *Top of the Pops* and all they ever showed was a picture [of] me," says Judge Dread.

From "Big 6":

> Little Boy Blue, come blow your horn.
> The sheep's in the meadow, the cows in the corn
> Ai yai ya …
> Where is the boy who looks after the sheep?
> He's under the haystack with Little Bo Peep
> Ai yai ya …
> Little Miss Muffet, sat on her tuffet
> Her knickers all tattered and torn.
> It wasn't a spider who sat down beside her —
> Was Little Boy Blue with the horn.

From "Big 7":

> Jack and Jill
> Went up a hill
> To fetch a roll of cheese.
> Jack came down
> With a scheming smile
> And his trousers round his knees.

So of course all of a sudden, I've become the biggest selling artist and I was above everybody — Elton John, Rod Stewart, even Elvis I think came fourth in that year. This is from somebody who nobody even knew what he looked like. It was incredible. I've never been on *Top of the Pops*.

I've sold in the U.K. now over 20 million records and if you think about it, I've packed stadiums out everywhere and it's just a cult following. It's sort of word of mouth that I've become, well they've put me in the *Guinness Book of World Records* as the world's first white toaster; I hold the highest number of banned hit records in the world; I had the first Ethiopian record in 1973; and there's another one they've got me down for, for another world record as well, all musical feats. I was selling 78,000 a day with "Big 7." "Big 7" is now in the top 500 of the biggest selling singles of all time.

But ska and reggae had their ups and downs in the U.K. in the '70s, so Judge Dread had to adapt to survive. And so he did, with his own unique genre. "I was actually playing gigs at the same time with all of our glam rockers, like Slade and Sweet and Gary Glitter and everything else. I was in the same vein. I was actually a pop star. What it actually meant was that during this time I managed to keep the music alive, when the music had died. By putting in my own brand and inventing what is now known as white reggae, I actually created white reggae, I've always called it Cockney reggae, we call it Dread Rock actually, because it's a music all its own. It's the only music there is. I use sort of orientated black backings, from people like the Cimarons and people like that, with a Cockney singer," he says.

Some critics of Judge Dread contend he was a novelty act, but novelties, by definition, do not last, and Judge Dread sustained for decades due to his adaptability, while staying true to form. "It's sort of held on over the years, which then made me the first punk because back in the day I was singing about ganja when people were still calling it pot. Afterwards with the punk era, once again, I became involved in that because I was already very anti-establishment. I was saying that I didn't like the queen and everything else that went with it. I was putting the national anthem on record and naughty rhymes along with it with 'Big 9,' which was one of my tracks. I actually had to have the record pressed in Holland because [of] EMI, which had the biggest pressing manufacturers here but wouldn't press it because I used the national anthem and they said it was in bad taste," he says.

Judge Dread admits it was tough sometimes being pigeonholed by the type of music he produced, but he understands that his own brand of ska was what he did best.

That's how it used to be in those days. Of course, once again now, right up to this date that still stands. Whatever I do, I'm still tarred with the same brush because I was the first to do this type of thing. I've always been considered, even though lots of things have come in bad taste or in very bad taste, it doesn't matter. Because I was the first, I've always been assumed to be the worst. We've got some terrible things, even some records that are played on the radio now. I mean all my stuff is basically innuendoes and these now, the load of the stuff, is absolutely horrendous. Judge Dread was the first and it's given me a bit of notoriety that nobody else in the music business would ever equal and in a way, okay, it's not a thing to be proud of, but at least I'm there. I'm in the *Guinness Book of World Records* and no one will ever take my records away, 'cause I've sold, in one country alone, over 20 million records without the aid of airplay on TV. Now no one will ever do that again. There is no word of mouth anymore. So I've got an unparalleled record there.

They've also put me down in the *Guinness Book of Musical Feats*. Actually, I'm the only person ever to be banned by the *Guinness Book of World Records* because at one time they thought it was in bad taste to put Judge Dread in there and I got an official ban from the *Guinness Book of Records*, which also made me another record holder. It's incredible. The other one they're putting me in there for is the World's Most Successful White Solo Reggae Artist. I've got the respect of the whole of the reggae world because they know that during that sort of bad period, from '71 and '75, '76, nothing was happening. Reggae had died as we know it.

The mid '70s were so tough, one of the biggest reggae labels, Trojan Records, went bankrupt and Judge Dread found himself in the strange position of having once been a debt collector for the same company that now owed him money. "In 1975, Trojan Records went bust and other than EMI, I was the second person they owed the most money to and they went down owing me sales of something like nine million records, which was over a million and a quarter, which in 1975 was a lot of money. A million and a quarter pounds we're talking here. That's probably like ten million pounds now, and they bounced a check on me about the same time for something like 386,000 (pounds), so of course I never got that," says Judge Dread. But he realized that he needed to be back in control of his own music rights, learned his lesson, and never looked back in these tough financial times. "I had made a deal with the liquidator, the guy in charge of the bankruptcy of Trojan, and I bought back my rights of all my hits for something like ten grand and that was it. So from that day onwards I've always controlled everything I do. I release on a non-exclusive basis and that's why I've successfully run my life. And it's been good," he says. "I've held onto it (reggae) until the 2Tone era came, so it's nice to actually be in there (the record books) for something."

The ska and reggae scene in the mid '70s in the U.K. may have experienced a slow down, but Judge Dread continued to record and perform. In 1973 he even organized Oxfam's Ethiopian Famine Appeal, a concert way before Live Aid's 1985 efforts. He recorded the official song of the concert, a cover of Clancy Eccles' "Molly" to help fund the work. Judge Dread's perseverance in tough times paid off, for in the late '70s, the 2Tone era came in like a cyclone and took the U.K. and the world by storm. Judge Dread's career was big again.

> All of the people, like the Madness boys and Bad Manners, they were all in school when I was actually recording. I was their hero. So when Madness was going to go into, when they first cut a demo of "Madness," the guy at the head of all the communications, Rob Dickens, he actually said to me, "Have a listen to this — what do you think?" And I said, "Oh god, it's terrible," because I'm still thinking black, I hear Madness and I'm thinking Prince Buster, and I hear "Madness, Madness, we call it Madness." It's a bunch of kids from Camden with a sooped-up tinny sound, and he said, "Do you fancy getting involved in this?" And I said no. I told the lads, Suggsy and the other boys, I said, "You're lucky I never touched it because I would've made it sound too good. I would've killed it." I would've killed 2Tone basically because the Dread stuff always has sort of a Jamaican orientated feel. I would've adapted a Jamaican feel to these lads from Camden town and I would've killed it, even though they were sort of big fans of mine, I let it be and somebody else picked up the bat, and there you go, they became big boys. It's the same with Bad Manners with Buster Bloodvessel. I was his hero when he was at school and it's strange because I'll go out and work with him.
>
> So of course when 2Tone struck in about '79, all of a sudden I found myself sort of moved on from my outfit of '70s shows and '70s people. My venues switched to 2Tone venues and there's a nouveau band of skinheads out there that I hadn't seen for nearly a decade. For 2Tone, the Dread thing sort of rose again on the musical round-a-bout. Around I went for another few years.

Like Laurel Aitken though, Judge Dread had a loyal following of skinhead fans that stayed true throughout the many eras of his career.

In 1975 when I thought it was the end of the skinhead thing, I actually wrote an album. The title was called *Judge Dread, Last of the Skinheads* and from that I wrote a song called "Bring Back the Skins." It's actually somebody lamenting that they don't play reggae too much in clubs and things like that. And unbeknownst to me, the new set of skinheads came out again and the passion, it's become the skinhead anthem now. It's absolutely huge. I do it and they cry. It makes them cry. A guy called James Hamilton who's a very very famous writer, he did one of the sleeve notes to one of these things one time and said it's the most authentic piece of sort of musical history he's ever heard. I'm just saying the music's not the same anymore. People don't dress the same, but at heart I'm still a skin.

One new element of the skinhead culture this time around, due in part to the political and social climate of economic strain and disenfranchisement was the presence of a racist faction of skinheads, very separate and different from the original skinhead movement. These racist skinheads, ironically, were also drawn to the Jamaican music and ska and reggae era in the U.K. during the 2Tone years. And Judge Dread remembers this time and says the media coverage during during this period contributed to the problem, greatly affecting his career.

I pulled out a bit because we had a problem here where it began to get very political, and I had a 14-piece band with fifty-fifty, seven Jamaicans and seven whites. All of a sudden the media started making them [the audience as portrayed on TV] lift up their hands in the air, like instead of going "skinhead, skinhead," it was "sieg heil, sieg heil," but it wasn't. The reporter would say there were people siegheiling there and then I got a couple of cancellations from various councils saying, "Well we can't have this because it's racist." How can Judge Dread be a racist? He's got seven blacks in his band! Some of me best friends included Bob Marley! It's absolutely ridiculous, so sooner than get into the confrontation over it, I actually pulled the band from the road and went into disco a while and went into making disco records. And during the '80s I sort of crossed over into dance music. All innuendoes again, a sort of tongue-in-cheek gesture.

So he didn't change his music completely, he just adapted it. And the association with racism was something Judge Dread took very personally, for his friends, enough to move away from the music he loved, until the situation subsided. "There is something people will never seem to understand. They associate skinheads with fascists and political this and that and the other. They don't realize, it's a musical breed. These people just follow the music. These kids travel miles and miles, just for their music. They support it. How can you be racists when the artists are black and the audience is white?" he says.

Judge Dread continued to perform and record, even in times when reggae and ska were out of favor. He was loyal to his fans until the end. On March 13, 1998, Judge Dread performed in Canterbury, England. After performing a rousing set at the Penny Theatre, Judge Dread told the crowd, "Let's hear it for the band," and fell on the stage. He was pronounced dead at the hospital from a massive heart attack, dead at only 53 years of age.

Alex Hughes lived like he died — an energetic performer who never gave up and carried the torch of ska and reggae through difficult times that may have seen most performers give up. Hughes was a big man in many ways. He was physically large and his confidence, determination, and skill were also big. But biggest was his heart, his love of the music and for those who enjoyed it.

CHAPTER SIX

Too Much Too Young: The Specials'
Roddy Radiation

THE SEVEN BLOKES TAKE THE STAGE and with a roll of the drums, jump into a frenetic performance, leaping like fish out of water in their tonic suits, black shoes with white socks, and pork pie hats around the dead-pan, eye-linered lead singer who looks straight into the camera like a hypnotist. The audience pogos and skanks and by the end of the show they are mesmerized and have joined their mates up on stage, the band called the Specials, whose leader and keyboardist Jerry Dammers declares, "Nobody Is Special!" because they see no boundary between band and audience, no separation between those who are elevated onto a stage and those who are part of the masses, and certainly no difference between black and white. With their music and their words, this group of dissimilar and often sparring seven boys from Coventry, England, changed the culture, politics, and music of their people, by bringing awareness and energy into a tumultuous and violent time.

Coventry, England, was a working-class city built upon the labor of the auto factories. And like Detroit, the motor city that begat Motown, so too did Coventry, a motor city, give birth to 2Tone, the label synonymous with English ska. 2Tone was started by Jerry Dammers, the Specials' keyboardist with the two missing front teeth. Dammers was born on May 22, 1954, in India as Gerald Dankey, but during the punk era in England, he changed his name to Jerry Dammers. His father was a reverend and his mother was an English teacher, and when Dammers was two years old, his family moved to Sheffield, England. There the family lived until Dammers was 10 years old when they moved to Coventry.

Dammers took an interest in music early in life and remembers his first introduction to Prince Buster's music at age 10 when Dammers' brother's friend played a copy of "Al Capone." When Dammers was 13 he took piano lessons, although he felt forced by his parents to take the lessons, and he soon quit since he disliked the instruction. Dammers also sang in his father's church choir, which he detested. Still, the musical introduction must have impacted the young Dammers who became a lifetime musician.

When Dammers was 15, he identified with a number of counterculture groups. This was during 1970s in England when counterculture groups were abundant. Dammers considered himself a mod and even a hippie and went to a commune on a small island off the coast of Ireland owned by John Lennon. But Dammers hated the shared work concept and left to become a skinhead, leaving school behind as well.

Dammers' brother became a doctor and his sister became a social worker, but Dammers chose not to pursue the university as they did and instead he found his calling in art. He enrolled in art school at Nottingham Art School. After only one year there, he left and attended Lanchester Polytechnic, an art and film school in Coventry. Dammers continued to usurp authority while at school, committing numerous acts of vandalism, smashing windows and drinking, resulting in arrests and court appearances. He produced three films while attending school, utilizing his skill for animation that would soon be employed to create a legendary logo and concept. Although Dammers completed all of the projects and curriculum for his art degree, he bucked authority once again by not even showing up to receive his degree at graduation or anytime after.

But Dammers was influenced by those he recognized as having abilities he admired. At a young age he heard music by the likes of the Kinks and the Small Faces, and soul artists like Sam & Dave, Otis Redding, and artists on the Motown label. In addition to Prince Buster, Dammers also listened to Desmond Dekker growing up, first hearing his reggae sounds in 1969 since West Indian culture was strong in the immigrant communities of England.

Dammers couldn't help but blend his love for reggae and soul with the dominant sound of British youth of his day, punk music, and when he played in a number of bands before forming the Specials, bands like Ricky Nugent and the Loiterers, the Ray King Soul Band (Charlie "H" Bembridge — sometimes called Aitch, and Neol Davies of the Selecter and Lynval Golding of the Specials also played with Ray King early in their careers), Peggy Penguin and the Southside Greeks, and the Sissy Stone Soul Band, Dammers was influenced by his passion. But it wasn't until he formed the Coventry Automatics, the band whose name would change to become the Specials, that Dammers brought his unique blend of reggae and punk into the studio and on stage. Dammers began experimenting with this fusion of reggae and punk, collaborating with fellow musician Neol Davies who later went on to record with the Selecter. Dammers and Davies put together demo tapes of early versions of songs that became classics of the Specials.

Key to the culture that launched English ska was Horace Panter, bass player for the Specials, born on August 30, 1953, as Stephen Graham Panter and also known as Sir Horace Gentleman, his stage name. Panter too was gifted at art and went through a one-year art program at Northampton School. Although Panter met many musicians in his art career, none were as beneficial as the connection he had at his next art school, Lanchester Polytechnic, where he met and befriended Jerry Dammers in 1973. While students there, Panter and Dammers collaborated together on a film before collaborating together on a new genre of music. But Dammers and Panter went separate ways after art school and didn't regroup until Dammers saw Panter play in Coventry. Panter was in a band called Breaker and Dammers asked Panter to play bass for some songs he had written, songs that were strongly influenced by Dammers' love for reggae.

Critical to that reggae sound was the next member of the band that Dammers assembled. Lynval Fitzgerald Golding knew reggae well since he was born in Jamaica on July 7, 1952. Golding grew up in an impoverished area in the parish of St. Catherine in a district called Mendez. The district had no electricity and no running water and Golding says his upbringing on the family farm was tough, but full of love and music. When Golding was only 10 years old his mother sent him and his sisters to live with his aunt in England so they could have a better life than she could provide.

Although Golding was unhappy at first in England, his family moved from town to town to find the right fit, from Southampton to Birmingham to Gloucester and then finally to Coventry. In England and especially from his schoolmates, Golding experienced racist taunts, something of which Golding was not familiar with in Jamaica. As a result, Golding hated school and became determined to stop the injustice he felt.

Lynval Golding, rhythm guitarist and backing vocals for the Specials, performs at the Metro in Chicago in 1998. He was born in Jamaica and moved to England at age 10, the same year he bought his first guitar (photograph Heather Augustyn).

The foundation for Golding's musical tastes was set as a child in Jamaica. Golding listened to the early ska and reggae pioneers of the 1950s and 1960s, including Derrick Morgan, Prince Buster, and Byron Lee and the Dragonaires, in addition to a local DJ called Mr. Green Sound System which brought the latest sounds to the people. In England, Golding continued to foster his love for music, enjoying the work of the Beatles, the Rolling Stones, Jimi Hendrix, and B.B. King.

At age 16, Golding left behind what he hated, school, and turned to what he loved, music. When he was just 10 years old he bought a Fender guitar with money he saved up by working odd jobs and so he put the guitar to use in his first band, the Merrytones. Golding relied on his taste for soul music and his band played mostly covers of soul artists, such as Sam & Dave and Otis Redding. Golding achieved success as a guitarist in Coventry although his father hoped his son would choose a career not based in the arts. So to appease him, Golding worked as an apprentice for an auto mechanic. Still, he pursued his dream — to be a musician. He left the Merrytones and joined a group that put him in contact with future members of the Selecter. The band, Pharaoh's Kingdom, included Charley Anderson, Desmond Brown, and Charlie "H" Bembridge. Golding's next stop with the Ray King Soul Band put him in touch with Jerry Dammers, although the two didn't play together in the band at the same time. They lived four doors away from each other and met at the local pub called The Pilot and they hit it off, especially since they had so much in common.

Golding was in the band the Automatics, along with Panter, Dammers, and Tim Strickland, a vocalist Dammers knew from a record store in Coventry, and Silverton Hutchinson, a drummer originally from Barbados that Dammers knew from his social circles. They began rehearsing under the direction of organizer Jerry Dammers. The Automatics, then called the Coventry Automatics since they found there was already a band called the Automatics signed to a record label, performed reggae and punk, a concoction that Dammers had masterminded for years. But the blend didn't mesh so well at first, and the Coventry Automatics played a residency on Monday nights at a club called Mr. George's, oscillating between genres — a few punk songs followed by a few reggae songs. Audiences were confused. The group decided they had to find a better match for their ideal sound, and so they ousted Strickland, who wasn't the right fit, and instead found a 17-year-old who also shared a love for ska and rhythm and blues, and serendipitously had just left his post as lead singer of a punk band, the Squad.

Terry Hall was born on March 19, 1959, and grew up in Coventry, the son of working class parents employed in the auto industry. Hall hated school and even tried to break his arm by jumping off a wall, just to get out of classes. He left school as soon as he could with no real plans for a job or a future. After trying out a number of different forms of employment, including working in a stamp shop, he turned to music and joined a band, the Squad. When he left the Squad, Dammers signed him up and his expressionless punk-era style of singing became the trademark voice of the Coventry Automatics and then the Specials.

The flavor of the band was added before the band continued their quest. Roddy Byers, known by the stage name Roddy Radiation, was recruited to play lead guitar since he was also a friend to Dammers. Byers was born in Coventry on May 5, 1955. His father introduced Byers to

music since he too was a musician. "My father played trumpet in a soul and blue beat band [ska is frequently called blue beat in England] in the late '60s, so I came from a musical background," says Byers. His father, Stan Byers, had a successful career and encouraged his son's love for music. But after school, Byers gained employment as a painter, only playing his guitar in his time off. He played at local clubs and in the early '70s he joined a band with Dammers called the Dread Rissoles, (a rissole is a meat-filled pastry), but both played different instruments at the time — Dammers played drums while Byers played bass. In 1975, Byers took up with a different band called the Wild Boys that featured Pete Davies who would later go on to play drums with the U.K. Subs. "My band, the Wild Boys, were a Coventry punk-rock-'n'-roll band which split in

Roddy Byers, better known as Roddy Radiation, lead guitarist for the Specials, was introduced to ska music by his father, who was a trumpeter in a blue beat band in England. Roddy performed with the Specials during their 30th Reunion Tour and continues to perform with his own band, the Skabilly Rebels (photograph courtesy Joe Kerrigan).

1977 and Jerry Dammers asked me to join to punk up his band who became the Specials," Byers says. Byers knew Hall as well, since Hall's band, the Squad, was an opening band for Byers' the Wild Boys. Byers did have a love for punk music, but also was a true fan of rockabilly and was a good music writer, having already penned the tune "Concrete Jungle," which he brought with him to the Specials. But ska wasn't in Byers' repertoire before he joined the ranks. "I had gotten into reggae through Bob Marley, but wasn't into ska pre–Specials. It mixed better with our punk-rock style than the reggae that we had played when the Automatics first formed, as it was rhythm-and-blues based and faster," Byers says.

Together, the group of Jerry Dammers on keyboards, Horace Panter on bass, Lynval Golding on rhythm guitar, Terry Hall on vocals, Silverton Hutchinson on drums, and Roddy Byers on lead guitar made up the Coventry Automatics, and Dammers had big dreams for them. One of those dreams involved securing Johnny Rotten from the newly disbanded Sex Pistols to join the group. So he set out for London, demo tapes in hand, but instead the demo tapes ended up with a roadie for the Sex Pistols and the Clash, Steve Connolly (also known as Rodent), who passed them along to Clash manager Bernie Rhodes. Connolly had also worked for the Wild Boys and knew Byers. Rhodes loved their sound and gave them a break that sealed their success — he sent them on the road with the Clash, opening for them on their 1978 "On Parole" tour, filling in for the band Suicide.

It was during this tour that Neville Staple was added to the mix. Staple, a roadie for the Coventry Automatics, began toasting over their songs during the very first night on tour and never stopped. Staple was born on April 11, 1955, in Christiana, Jamaica. He left Jamaica when he was five years old and moved to England. Staple was rebellious even in the early days of his youth, and a handful for his strict family, running away from home, skipping school to watch porn films at an adult theatre, and stealing money from his job at a grocery store to buy a scooter. But music was always a solid foundation for Staple. He grew up in a household where his parents listened to ska, or as they called it in England, blue beat. And the music was more than just something the family turned on every now and then — it was a way of life. He was born into this music and it was part of his culture.

When Staple was a teenager in England, he ran his own sound system, just like the ones he heard growing up in Jamaica. Staple and his sound system partner, Trevor Evans, always wanted a bigger sound to compete, so they robbed houses to get cash and both ended up in prison for six months. After he got out, he continued to DJ, playing at clubs where he ran into the members of the Coventry Automatics. He attended some of their gigs and eventually became their roadie. He joined the band officially as a vocalist during the Clash tour, providing a perfect counterpart sound to Hall. Whereas Hall's style was punky and emotionless, yet full of aloof attitude, Staple was raw energy, sprinkling in just enough spice to make each song perfectly palatable.

Bernie Rhodes only paid the Coventry Automatics £25 a night to perform, and with seven members, that amount wasn't enough even for decent sleeping arrangements in a hotel, so they slept in a tent that the Clash's tour manager lent them. When the Clash found out what Rhodes was paying their supporting band, they insisted he double their pay, which is what he did. The Clash members were close with the members of the Coventry Automatics, especially since Staple was Mick Jones's supplier of marijuana on the tour.

Self-proclaimed rude boy Neville Staple, backing vocalist for the Specials, performs at the infamous Metro show in Chicago in 1998. Staple began his work with the Specials as their roadie (photograph Heather Augustyn).

After the tour, the band went through a line-up change, as well as their name change. Silverton Hutchinson made his departure from the band when he decided he didn't want to play ska. As a reggae drummer with his interest in roots reggae, Hutchinson felt ska was too retro and not to his liking. When Dammers asked him to play differently, Hutchinson, who was known to have a temper, packed up his drums and simply left. The rest of the band chose to replace Hutchinson with John Bradbury, also known as Brad. Bradbury was a friend of those in the group as well as a housemate to Dammers in 1975. The band also changed their name when they found out there was another band called the Automatics playing and they feared their name might be confused. So they changed the name to the Special A.K.A. the Coventry Automatics, which was deemed too awkward, so they simply called themselves the Specials.

Bernie Rhodes continued to manage the band after the tour dates and he gave the Specials some advice that would shape the look and entire image of English ska. Dammers contends that Rhodes suggested an image for the band, a band comprised of both black and white musicians. They needed a cohesive, marketable look. Dammers says he took the black and white checkerboard from tape that decorated his bike when he was a mod, and used it in their materials. This black and white came to symbolize the unity of black and white races, for the band, the listeners of the music, and the social composition of late 1970s England. The band members also punctuated their look with tonic suits, white socks, black shoes, and the image was born.

Dammers, an illustrator from his days at art school, designed a logo to go along with their new look. He drew a dapper man in a suit and pork-pie hat, very similar to the rude boy look of 1960s Jamaica, known as Walt Jabsco, a moniker he assigned from one of his own used bowling shirts. The illustration was based upon a photo of Peter Tosh that is the cover of the Wailing Wailers album, although the similarity is fairly scant. Walt Jabsco became the mascot for English ska, and black and white checks became a symbolic design on English ska materials.

The relationship with Rhodes was fruitful, but didn't last long since Dammers and Rhodes were two strong personalities and Dammers wanted to call the shots. Rhodes did allow the Specials to reside at the Clash's studio at Chalk Farm, north of London, but that too lasted a short time since it was cold and infested with rats. After a final gig in Paris, Rhodes was gone. But this gig inspired one of the Specials' most classic songs, "Gangsters," a song that became their first single and started it all.

The Specials stayed at a hotel in Paris that had just been host to the Damned. The hotel proprietors claimed the Damned had caused damage to the hotel, so the hotel staff took two guitars owned by members of the Specials to cover the cost. Golding and Byers were without their guitars, but when the manager of the club turned up at the hotel to sort it out, after some pushing and shoving, he told the band to report to the club. When they did, all of their equipment, including the guitars, was there waiting. When the owner of the club came to greet the band, he opened up his jacket to offer Hall a mint, and inside, very visible, they all saw a gun. The man was a member of the French mafia, and thus the opening line of "Gangsters," and the rest of the song about the experience resulted.

The Specials knew they were marketable and talented, so Dammers approached Rough Trade, the biggest indie record label at the time in England, and presented "Gangsters." Rough Trade loved the song and agreed to produce 5,000 copies, even though Dammers only had set a goal for 2,500 copies. The band then borrowed £700 for the production. The DIY project found the members of the Specials stamping their own labels on each individual plain white record sleeve. They were almost ready to hit the public, but there was a little problem — what to record on the B side of the single. The Specials had simply run out of money and couldn't afford any more studio time, so Golding contacted his good friend and colleague Neol Davies, a guitarist, and secured an instrumental Davies, Golding, and Bradbury had recorded at Davies' home the previous year. The song, "The Selecter," became the B side of the single, as well as the name of Davies' future band.

The single became an immediate huge hit. John Peel, the famous English DJ, invited the group in studio to play for his famous "sessions" and broadcast the Specials live on Radio One. As a result, the band was booked for live performances everywhere. During one of those performances in early May 1979, at the Moonlight Club venue in London, Mick Jagger attended to hear the Specials, the band that was getting all the buzz. He liked what he heard and wanted to sign the band to Rolling Stone Records, but the Specials had also caught the attention of numerous other record executives and Dammers was careful to keep control and not sell out to just anyone. After all, Dammers was a rebel in charge.

The band, now rid of Rhodes, decided to sign with another manager and chose Rick Rogers, who also managed the Damned and was a housemate to a former teacher of Dammers and Panter back at Lanchester Polytechnic. Rogers continued to book the band at London venues and the Specials appeared on the same bill as the U.K. Subs and the Damned. All 5,000 copies of "Gangsters" had sold out and the Specials now realized they had huge negotiating power with the hordes of record companies knocking on their door. Despite having more lucrative deals on the table, Dammers and crew chose to have control over their own image and the autonomy of their own label, to a degree. They signed to Chrysalis Records with the understanding that the band would have their own separate sub label, or imprint, that they could then sign additional bands to at will. Roy Eldridge, Chrysalis's A&R man, responsible for artist development for the label, was so enthusiastic about the Specials he agreed to the deal, offering their label, which they aptly called 2Tone to represent the black and white image, the ability to record ten singles a year with a budget of £1000 per single. The band themselves signed to the Chrysalis label for five albums and more if the partnership went well. The deal the band just signed, and the launch of the band into the music business, was the spark of a powder keg for ska music in England.

Neol Davies was also part of these early negotiations and he quickly formed the Selecter to take advantage of the opportunity. All of the members of both bands, the Specials and the Selecter, were now directors of the 2Tone label under the agreement with Chrysalis. The Specials and the 2Tone label were now off and running. Chrysalis distributed an additional run of "Gangsters" with a new record sleeve adorned by the Walt Jabsco logo and black and white checkers. The song hit the top ten and the band performed on an eight-week tour of the U.K., as well as on the *Top of the Pops*, a British television show that featured live performances by the "it" bands who topped the charts. Performing on *Top of the Pops* was a sign of success for a band in England.

Jerry Dammers was eager to get the 2Tone label started and went to see his first band of interest, which he immediately liked and immediately signed. Madness became the second band signed to 2Tone with their single "The Prince." The song, a nod to Prince Buster, went to the top 20 in England. The two bands then went on tour together to promote their new sound. Madness opened for the Specials in June 1979, and they performed under a banner that stated "The Rude Boys Return," an acknowledgment of their Jamaican roots and the hint of a new era. Crowds were so large that many fans were turned away at the doors and music critics gave rave reviews of the performances. The Specials and Madness continued to tour together, appearing at a music festival called the Bilzen Jazz and Rock Festival in Belgium with other bands such as the Police, the Pretenders, AC/DC, and the Cure.

Meanwhile, back in England, the Selecter recorded their first release for 2Tone. "On My Radio" became the third single for the ska label with the charismatic Pauline Black on vocals ranking in the top ten.

The Specials were ready to strike while the iron was hot so they went into the studio to record their second single, the fourth for the 2Tone label. The song, "A Message to You Rudy" was a cover of the Dandy Livingstone song, "Rudy, A Message to You," which experienced popularity in 1967 in Jamaica. Because Jamaican ska was based in brass, the Specials added brass to their lineup by bringing in Rico Rodriguez on trombone and Dick Cuthell on coronet. Rico was a true Jamaican ska legend and had played trombone on the Livingstone original version of the song, as well as performing with such Jamaican greats as the Skatalites, Prince Buster, and Laurel Aitken.

Rico was born Emmanuel Rodriguez in the Matthew Lane neighborhood on the west side of Kingston, Jamaica, on October 17, 1934. Like many Jamaican musicians of his time, Rodriguez attended the Alpha Boys School from 1940 until 1954. Rodriguez studied under the tutelage of genius trombonist Don Drummond who served as Rodriguez's tutor in school. While in his last two years at Alpha Boys School, Rodriguez worked as an apprentice to a mechanic, but realizing his true love was music, he continued his music education after school and attended Roland Alphonso's alma mater, Stony Hill Music School from 1955–1957.

Also like many other Jamaican musicians in this era, Rodriguez cut his musical chops at Studio One as a session musician for Clement "Coxsone" Dodd. In fact, Rodriguez performed for the first studio session Coxsone arranged in 1956, recording the trombone part for the classic ska song, "Easy Snappin'" by Theophilus Beckford, and other songs by Clue J and the Blues Blasters. Yet another similarity with other Jamaican musicians was Rodriguez's performances for the Eric Dean Orchestra and the Jamaica Jazz Orchestra, as well as competing at the *Vere Johns Opportunity Hour* at the Palace Theatre in Kingston, at which Rodriguez won many awards. He performed for a number of Jamaican artists and producers as a studio musician, including The Skatalites alongside Don Drummond, Vincent Chin, Duke Reid, Stanley Motta with Derrick Harriott, and the Jiving Juniors.

Rodriguez associated with the Rasta community and began attending Count Ossie's Rasta Camp in East Kingston in the Wareika Hills. Rodriguez went there as a teenager in the late 1950s, following his mentor, Don Drummond, who also went to the camp. The apprentice-like relationship was so close that when Drummond composed his songs, Rodriguez even drew the music staffs onto the blank sheets for him. He learned most of what he knew as a musician from living at the camp with other musicians and experienced musical exploration and experimentation unlike any other environment could provide. Here too he was able to live among like-minded people and enjoyed a shared spirituality and a lifestyle that provided sustenance and fulfillment. Rodriguez never required much to live and played his trombone in order to have food to eat, frequently performing on the docks where the fishing boats returned, playing for fish, in order to survive.

Rodriguez then moved to London in 1962 to try to make a better living. He met Laurel Aitken, who introduced him to Shalit, owner of Melodisc Records in England, and co-owner of Blue Beat Records with Prince Buster. Rodriguez recorded for the Blue Beat label for three years, as well as recording for Pama Records, a label owned by brothers Harry, Jeff, and Carl Palmer. It was on this label Rodriguez released his album, "Rico In Reggaeland," in 1967.

In addition to giving Rodriguez his musical skill and spirituality, Count Ossie's camp also inspired Rodriguez's best-known song and album, "Man From Wareika," recorded in Jamaica and released in 1976 for Island Records, Chris Blackwell's label. This album, entirely instrumental, is credited with bridging the gap between reggae and jazz since it was released in the U.S. by Blue Note, a jazz label. Although jazz and ska are inextricably linked due to their roots, and reggae as a derivative of ska is thereby linked to jazz by association, it wasn't until Rodriguez's album that the link was made by U.S. record executives, providing an entirely new audience for the music. Rodriguez also gained another new audience with this album release — the world, as he toured Europe in support of Bob Marley on his Exodus tour and was finally a full-time musician, earning much more than just fish.

It was because of Rodriguez's talent and background that the Specials wanted to add him to their lineup. Rodriguez says that his daughter received phone calls everyday that the Specials were looking for him and wanted him to join their band. But Rodriguez, always an independent musician, didn't want to join their band because he feared his career would disappear into obscurity once the band broke up. But he did agree to record with them, as well as tour with them for two years before the Specials did indeed break up. "Working with Rico was like working with a very cool grandparent! And as he'd played on the original 'A Message to You Rudy,' it gave us credibility. I would often ask him for advice on my personal problems and we would often gather at his feet in different hotel rooms while he gave forth his wisdom and read to us from his Bible. We would also smoke quite a lot of ganja. Dick Cuthell and Rico gave a touch of musical class to our punky/ska," says Byers.

The timing of the song "A Message to You Rudy," was as appropriate in late 1970s England as it was in 1960s Jamaica. An energetic, largely unemployed, struggling youth found anger an easy emotional response to the socially difficult times in the devastating Margaret Thatcher-driven government. This song was a message for these angry youth to calm down and to not turn to violence, a theme that would return throughout the 2Tone era. The B side of "A Message to You Rudy," featured the classic tune "Nite Klub," a sardonic criticism of trendy club life with the in-crowd.

With the success of two singles and the 2Tone label launched, the time had come for the Specials to release their own album and so they went into the studio. Many of the songs were written by various members of the band, but Dammers served as the group's leader since he founded the group, and since he had the personality for it.

One critical person who got his influence in on the Specials' debut and self-titled album was producer Elvis Costello. Dammers contends that Costello approached them and asked if he could produce their album and they obliged. Byers remembers, "He did come to lots of our early gigs and was better than some middle-of-the-road producer as he understood our politics and also he was an intermediary between the old school and the new. We all loved his first album and he seemed a nice guy in a sort of Woody Allen kind of way." Drawing upon the past year of live performances, the Specials recorded at TW Studios in Fulham, England, whose facilities were small and dank, but afforded a tight-knit creativity unlike any other. Dammers says that the band was drunk during most of the recording of this album since they all frequented the pub across the street from the studio.

The result, however, was magic, but not necessarily chemistry, especially between Costello and Byers. Costello expressed to Dammers that he should find a new lead guitarist since Byers' style was too rockabilly, he felt. And Byers felt that Costello never really understood the Specials' sound and instead thought it was reggae, a heavy section, and reggae again, without the blend. "Elvis told the band to sack me because he couldn't see a punk rock 'n' roll guitarist fitting in. He missed the whole point as we weren't reviving Jamaican ska but taking it somewhere else. Since then, it's been said I started ska punk! But that's the only way I could play at that particular time," said Byers. Nevertheless, the album was a huge success, entering album charts at number seven and producing two top ten hits, "Gangsters," and "Too Much Too Young."

Even though Costello's run at producer for the Specials was over, his experience with the 2Tone label was not. Costello's own sound in 1979 was largely influenced by his days spent with the Specials and the prominent ska sound of the time. In late 1979, Elvis Costello and the Attractions recorded their *Get Happy!* album, but due to a dispute with Warner Brothers, Costello's label, he had no one to put out the album. Eager to capitalize on the trend and get his music heard, Costello and Dammers agreed to have 2Tone release Costello's single, "I Can't Stand Up For Falling Down," a hipster remake of the Sam & Dave tune from two decades earlier. It was a one-time release and is a collector's item today.

The Specials continued to sign other bands to the 2Tone label, such as the all-girl band the Bodysnatchers, the Beat, the Special A.K.A (comprised of post break-up Specials' members and Rhoda Dakar of the Bodysnatchers), the Apollinaires, the Higsons, J.B.'s Allstars, the Friday Club, Rico as a solo artist, and the Swinging Cats. In the seven years the 2Tone label existed, they released 29 singles and eight albums.

If there are two halves of the Specials, a black and a white perhaps, then the other half of the Specials' music and career is certainly the social times in which they were playing and their message and response to that condition. The British economy in the late 1970s and early 1980s, as driven by Prime Minister Margaret Thatcher, was in shambles. By 1982, unemployment in England was the highest since the 1930s, doubling since Thatcher took office a few years earlier. Dave Wakeling of 2Tone's the Beat remembers,

> There was a recession, or perhaps a depression in the late '70s, who knows, and so division reared its ugly head. There were movements like the British Movement and the National Front which were white supremacist organizations that were feeding on the frustrations and the energy of the white skinheads who mainly inhabited the soccer terraces, but also liked ska music. The skinheads were the first people who got into reggae which we always thought was odd, or not odd, but ironic at least and so there was this pull. Unemployment was high, 17%, probably higher in minority circles, and so they went for ability, for extreme right-wing organizations, to try to feed on this youth frustration. And although it didn't happen on purpose, the Beat, the Specials, and the Selecter found ourselves playing to multi-racial audiences in the industrial Midlands where the white skinheads were now being targeted by all the shadowy right-wing organizations that were trying to get them as their storm troopers.

Roddy Byers says the rise of these racist groups, their presence at their shows, and the economic condition of England at the time was a part of their music. "Unemployment and racism were rife at the time we formed, and being a multi-racial band, we could not ignore the rise of fascist parties like the National Front. Some of us were socialist too and disliked Margaret Thatcher's right-wing policies," says Byers. "Much has been said about the so-called National Front problems, but it didn't happen that often. Sometimes it was just skinheads from different towns fighting over soccer teams. But on occasion we were targeted, like the time we played 'Rock Goes to College' for the BBC TV at Colchester and the Nazi skinheads smashed our tour bus windows in while we were playing a concert. We drove home to Coventry sitting in broken glass, very cold, as it was winter time," Byers says.

For the black members of the group, the racist presence at their performances was too real and very personal. Sometimes, National Front members who ironically came to the Specials' shows would give Nazi salutes to the members of the band and then begin throwing pennies and coins at Neville Staple and Lynval Golding. They also spit on the black members of the band.

Racist violence for the Specials was so rough that Lynval Golding himself became the subject of a racist attack in 1980 outside the Hampstead Moonlight Club. Golding was walking down the road with two white girls when a group of racist thugs beat him up so badly that they broke several of his ribs. Golding, determined not to let the criminals affect him or his band's success, endured injections of painkillers in order to perform the next day at the famous Montreaux Jazz Festival. He was attacked again in 1982 in Coventry City Centre, stabbed several times in the neck by racist criminals. He nearly died, as the knife came close to his jugular vein, and he was in intensive care for days. Golding wrote the song, "Why?" whose lyrics point out the stupidity of racism.

But the founding values of the Specials, the blend of Jamaica and England, the mix of black and white, and the devotion to unity, persevered. The band members always stood together and represented unity. "Coventry was and is a mixed race city and it wasn't that unusual for black and white musicians to play together, and the punk rock scene like in London included a fair amount of reggae music. But we didn't really feel that aware of it until we started playing other towns and cities throughout the U.K. and when the press and other musicians commented on the black and white mixture. All white musicians I knew loved black music, as all the music forms we were into originate from black American music," says Byers.

The lyrics of the Specials' songs carried their message, pointing out the absurdity of racism and violence. On their first album, released in October 1979, the song, "Do the Dog," opens with the following lyrics:

All you punks and all you teds
National Front and Natty Dreads
Mods, rockers, hippies, and skinheads
Keep on fighting 'till you're dead.

Numerous songs recorded by the members of the Special A.K.A. in the years following the breakup of the initial band also contained lyrics against racism and violence, such as the song "Racist Friend," written by Dammers, Dick Cuthell, the coronet player and friend to Rodriguez, and John Bradbury. The song was released in August 1983.

Violence, anger, and rioting were prevalent in England and the Specials couldn't ignore it. One of their greatest songs comes from this era, chronicling the effect of the violence and unemployment on the towns that once thrived. Coincidentally, the same week the song hit the radio waves in June 1981, riots broke out in Brixton and Liverpool, as well as in other small towns around England, and so the song, "Ghost Town," has become a memorial to these times and an anthem for what once occurred. Dammer's eerie guitar followed by Rico's and Cuthell's dooming brass convey the gravity of the situation.

"Jerry Dammers was the man behind 'Ghost Town' with a little help from Neville Staple and the rest of us, but it was mainly Jerry's baby. I don't think any of us realized how important the song would become to the history of the Specials. We had all seen how the country was getting run down, unemployment, and the youth getting angry when we were touring the U.K., but I don't think any of us thought it was such a powder keg waiting to explode into riots," Byers says.

In addition to songs that communicated to their audiences, the members of the Specials were also very politically and socially involved. "The Specials, being a multi-racial band with socialist leanings (some of us), played many cause-related shows, such as Rock Against Racism, benefits for unmarried mothers, UNICEF, anti-nuclear rallies, the list goes on and on," says Byers.

Most of the band's political activity, though, was done after the original line-up had left, and some of it was done by Dammers alone. Dammers helped to organize Artists Against Apartheid and was asked to head up the festival by Dali Tambo, the son of Oliver Tambo who was, at the time, the leader of the African National Congress in South Africa. The first concert, called Freedom Beat, took place on Clapham Common in London in 1986. Artists such as Peter Gabriel, Sting, Sade, the Smiths, and Big Audio Dynamite, Mick Jones's new band since the break-up of the Clash, performed. Some 250,000 people attended the concert which was preceded by a march to the concert grounds. After the success of Freedom Beat, a much bigger concert was organized to celebrate Mandela's 70th birthday, and so on June 11, 1988, a massive concert took place at Wembley Stadium. Some 72,000 people attended live at Wembley Stadium and more than 600 million people from 60 countries watched the broadcast on television. An enormous list of artists performed, including Stevie Wonder, Sly & Robbie, UB40, Harry Belafonte, Phil Collins, Whitney Houston, and Chrissie Hynde. Numerous celebrities attended and lent their support. Dammers' song, "Nelson Mandela," recorded by the Special A.K.A. in March 1984, brought attention to a hero who was previously considered a terrorist by the Tory government in England. Dammers wrote the song after attending a 65th birthday concert at Alexandria Palace in 1983. The song was produced, once again, by Elvis Costello and the Beat's Dave Wakeling and Ranking Roger sang backup vocals, along with other vocalists.

With so much talent, and so much popularity, it's hard to understand why the Specials broke up, dissolving their original lineup into other incarnations, after only two years. A combination of factors took their toll on the band members who were really just boys, experiencing too much too young. They were teenagers who thought the fame would never end.

Even though external politics were important to the members of the band and they drew together to deal with these issues, they simply were too young and too inexperienced to deal with the internal politics of seven band mates, each autonomous and each clamoring for a piece of the pie that had suddenly become very bountiful without much warning.

Byers has a conflicted respect for Dammers and is a musician with his own creative direction for the band that he feels was never given proper attention.

> Jerry Dammers was the man who had the vision and his determination got the band off the ground in the beginning. But he didn't like power sharing and tried to run everything himself. Our manager [Rick Rogers]

was just someone to interpret Jerry's ideas to the music business. I disagreed with the musical direction of our second album, *More Specials*, which Jerry wanted to be a Musak-lounge jazz experiment. I was moving in a completely different direction, fusing ska with rockabilly. This difference of opinion destroyed our friendship. But I wasn't the only one who wasn't keen on our leader's new musical direction. Jerry has refused to re-form the original band since 1981 and even now we as a band find it hard to communicate.

Certainly exhaustion was a major contribution to the communication breakdown and power struggles. The constant touring is cited by all members as a reason for their breakup. Touring prior to their album launch, recording their first album in the studio, followed by performances in Germany and then a massive tour in support of the album and the 2Tone label (the Specials, the Selecter, and Madness) was a whirlwind. The members spent most of their days drinking in order to cope with the mayhem and the violence and racism present at the shows only increased their stress levels. The Specials then performed on *The Top of the Pops* on November 7, 1979, and they continued their 2Tone tour with Dexy's Midnight Runners, who replaced Madness on the bill since Madness left to tour the U.S. and branch out on their own. Meanwhile, the 2Tone label was still booming as they signed the Beat by Christmas time. The Specials continued the pace, filming multiple shows for the BBC in January 1980. Meanwhile, the Elvis Costello single was recorded, and legal battles with Costello's label ensued. The Specials then released an EP and immediately took off on a tour of Europe, followed by their tour of the U.S., a test to see how American audiences would respond to the English ska craze. The Specials' manager, Rick Rogers, was responsible for organizing press conferences as well as booking hotels, none too flashy for Dammers' tastes, and one with 24-hour room service for Rico's food cravings at 2 A.M.

On January 24, 1980, the Specials' first played the U.S. in New York City and showed up two hours late for their gig. Still, the wall-to-wall crowd responded with enthusiasm. For the next three weeks, the Specials opened for the Police on their tour, traveling to places such as Boston, Oklahoma, Los Angeles, Seattle, New Orleans, and Vancouver and music critics gave the Specials a better review than they gave to the

Police. The last date on the Specials' tour of America, back in New York headlining at the Diplomat Hotel, was attended by Robert Smith of the Cure, David Bowie, the Go-Gos, Debbie Harry (Blondie), and even Mick Jagger who was still a fan of the Specials, despite having been turned down on his offer of a record deal.

But America was tough for the Specials, even though they had experienced popularity with the crowds. Lynval Golding experienced racism from a jewelry store owner in Chicago who refused him entry until he heard Golding's English accent, but by then, of course, it was too late. Dammers had a hard time with what he perceived as American commercialism and the country fawning over him. He refused to sit down for an early-morning interview by walking, hung over and fully clothed, into the hotel swimming pool. He also went into a rage when he discovered the Whiskey-A-Go-Go in Los Angeles was decorated in black and white checkers by employees of the club, but he thought it was a record label publicity stunt. Rico spent all night before traveling to Canada hiding his marijuana in his Bible, only to get busted by customs for possession — of an orange! And the tour, despite its success with American fans, still lost money. Chrysalis saw the band as an investment and spent a lot of money promoting the band and touring the band, frequently setting them up on two gigs per night.

"I think the main reason we didn't crack America was we hadn't had a break for a long time and had been on the road constantly. Also, reggae and punk were hardly accepted in America, let alone a strange mixture of the two with left wing leaning lyrics!" Byers says.

Back at home, the band signed the Bodysnatchers to the 2Tone label and the Specials continued touring Europe without a moment of rest. Their tour in France was particularly violent with racist skinheads in the audience, spitting and brawling with band members. After their merchandise was stolen or destroyed, the band packed up and headed for home. They then recorded more songs, appeared again on *Top of the Pops*, and went through more touring and more publicity, which only brought more stress. Golding went through a divorce and child-support litigation, and Dammers' long-time girlfriend left him as well. Fighting between Byers and Dammers occurred frequently, resulting in smashed equipment and smashed relationships. But still, the band continued their frenzied pace.

Saturday Night Live booked the band to perform on the show on April 19, 1980, so the group returned to America. Again, the American way of life was not to the Specials' liking. They refused the limo the show sent for their transportation and instead took a taxi. They also refused to perform in front of the *SNL* backdrop on the musician's stage, a photo of Rockefeller Center, saying it was a symbol of capitalism. But the members were very pro-consumption when it came to the after party with *SNL* cast and crew at John Belushi's bar. Rogers contends that he saw more alcohol and drugs that night than he had ever seen and ever will see. Byers recalls the experience, "I remember Jerry not being happy with the posh hotel and him wanting to use our performance politically, but most of us never really took TV seriously. It was just a chance to jump around and show off. Keith Richards turned up and said a few kind words to us all before and after the show, which seemed to panic the show's organizers even more. But I think the performance shows the manic kind of show we were doing at that particular time."

The band continued their touring and this time set out for Japan in July 1980, but the shows were mobbed with energetic fans that rioted at shows. When they returned to England, the band got word their friends and partners, the Selecter, had decided to leave the 2Tone label to pursue a contract directly with Chrysalis.

So the Specials, in an attempt to keep the success of ska and the 2Tone label going, went back in the studio to record a second album, the album that Byers said he felt had the wrong direction, as also felt by other members of the band. The album, *More Specials*, was an eclectic mix of everyone's stabs at songwriting. *More Specials* contained a song written by Terry Hall, some cover songs, experiments in Musak and electronica from Dammers, and more rockabilly mod from Byers. Horace Panter has described the album as the sound of the band breaking up. But still, the band had to promote the album and so they hit the road in England. Tensions in the band and with the audience had not dissipated in the studio and in Cambridge, a tussle between the audience and security at the venue resulted in Hall and Dammers spending the night in jail and a £400 fine for inciting a riot. The violence between the band and the audience was always a concern because of a tradition established by the band — to allow audience members up on the stage since the band didn't believe in a separation between performer and listener.

"Stage invasions — well it was fun to start with but as our crowds got bigger it got dangerous with stages collapsing and lighting rigs falling over, but once it started, it was very hard to stop," says Byers. The Specials helped set the stage for this tradition that continues in ska and punk today, from the Toasters to Iggy Pop.

The violent and energetic crowds and the exhaustion of touring was hard and now the band members were at their end. So the band, early in 1981, took a break from business in hopes of recharging their batteries. The decision was made by the entire group. While on their hiatus, however, band members continued working, albeit in individual ways. Neville Staple began his own record label, Shack Records, with the help of his Bodysnatchers girlfriend Stella Barker. The first band they signed, 21 Guns, included Johnny Rex and Trevor Evans, both Specials' roadies and Evans was Staple's friend from back in his DJ days when the two spent time in prison for stealing. John Bradbury too began his own record label, Race Records, and signed bands such as Team 23 and Night Doctor, the latter including Silverton Hutchinson, the Coventry Automatics' ex-drummer, as well as Charley Anderson and Desmond Brown, formerly of the Selecter. Roddy Byers began another band on the side called the Tearjerkers and Horace Panter joined a cult called Exegesis, leaving the band a short time after they all reconvened.

Dammers, meanwhile, took a brief vacation in Scotland and then put together a film about 2Tone called *Dance Craze*. The film ended up a document of live footage of 2Tone bands and wasn't very well received by movie goers who had hoped for something more substantive. Dammers also completed a single with Rhoda Dakar, ex-Bodysnatchers member, called "The Boiler" that was more akin to disco and told the first-person chronicle of a rape. Dammers said later of the song that it was only meant to be heard once. It was hardly a hit on the dance floor and some radio stations banned it due to its controversial nature, although it did get to number 32 on the charts.

But the project Neville Staple, Lynval Golding, and Terry Hall were working on, unbeknownst to Dammers, had the most impact on the rest of the band. They were planning an exit from the Specials. But still, the band convened after their rest to produce one of their greatest pieces of music, a last hurrah, "Ghost Town," which hit number one in the charts in June 1981. Even when they performed the tune on *Top of the Pops*, they were arguing backstage and it was here that Hall, Staple, and Golding told Dammers they were leaving the band.

Forming a new group called the Fun Boy Three, Hall, Staple, and Golding left for many reasons, first of which was they were fed up with touring. Manager Rick Rogers left the Specials as well to manage the Fun Boy Three. Dammers felt betrayed. Byers followed suit and put his time and energy into his other band, the Tearjerkers. "For most of us, it was a dream come true, to start with," says Byers of his time with the Specials. "But we had very little time off before the U.S. tour and we were pretty burned out. Due to tiredness, with two shows a night sometimes, we lost our love for each other and stopped communicating. The band toured constantly and we wore ourselves out, plus disagreement over musical direction and Jerry Dammers' 'benign dictatoring' made some of us want to try it on our own," says Byers.

The Fun Boy Three had some immediate success. Their first single, "The Lunatics Have Taken Over the Asylum," was recorded in three months and in November 1981 it made the top 20 list in England. They also recorded a single and B side, "T'Aint What You Do (It's the Way You Do It)"/"The Funrama Theme" with the popular all-girl band Bananarama. Their second album was produced by David Byrne of the Talking Heads, released on Chrysalis, as was their first album. Hall went on to form the Colour Field. And the Tearjerkers also proved successful for Byers. "I had formed a sideline band, the Tearjerkers, during a short break from the Specials' touring and left to pursue my interests in rockabilly, Cajun, and blues. We stayed together for seven years and put out a single, "Desire," and an EP on Chaswick Records. We had no major success as the fashion in the U.K. had changed to the New Romantics, which had little in common with my Socialist skabilly leanings," says Byers.

So Dammers was left to continue the band, whose lineup was always changing. Rhoda Dakar of the Bodysnatchers joined when she and her band mate Nicky Summers decided to leave their band. The rest of the girls in their original band founded the Belle Stars. Dammers renamed his group The Special A.K.A. Still under contract with Chrysalis, John

Bradbury, Rhoda Dakar, and Dammers decided to record a new album, so Dammers put together additional musicians, including Stan Campbell from the Selecter as vocalist and John Shipley of the Swinging Cats.

The album, appropriately titled *In the Studio*, took an excessive amount of time to produce, literally three years with extensive overdubbing and editing work. The band held no rehearsals or performances and instead they did all of their work in the studio, racking up huge bills that the sale of the album simply could never recoup. The album flopped and Dammers blamed its failure on lack of cooperation among band members instead of taking any ownership. Chrysalis refused to spend a lot of money on promotion, having already exhausted their supplies on production. Perhaps one of the only redeeming qualities of the album was the song "Nelson Mandela," which charted at number nine in March 1984 and led to an awareness of the South African leader. Other songs on the album took on weighty subjects with a brooding mood and were a far cry from the early ska days of the original sound.

After the major production with minor results, the existing band was exhausted. Campbell left the band and the rest of the members never performed live together. Dammers himself called the album, "the great mistake." After one last single, "The Alphabet Army," released by Dammers' loyal mate John Bradbury and his new band, J.B.'s All-Stars, the 2Tone label was finished for good. But as is often the case, great success is accompanied by ample failure. The 2Tone label may have had its share of failures at the end and even internally along the way. However, 2Tone was a huge success for the genre of ska, and for itself and the bands under its umbrella. From 1979 when the label was established until 1986 when it folded, 2Tone released 28 singles and 20 of them charted, in addition to releasing eight albums. More substantively though, the label shed light on important social issues, such as racism, unemployment, Apartheid, rape, violence, and war.

Since then, the Specials have re-formed in part, never with Dammers, but have recorded and toured. In fact, in 1996, a reduced lineup of the original band put out the album *Today's Specials* from Virgin Records that was a compilation of cover songs, and in 1998 the original lineup, minus Hall and Dammers, put out the album *Guilty 'Til Proved Innocent* on the MCA label.

In the U.S. on April 8, 1998, while on tour to promote *Guilty 'Til Proved Innocent* at the Metro in Chicago, Staple was arrested for battery against another band's lead singer who, according to Robert Preston (lead singer of the Cupcakes) told Staple where to put his equipment and Staple argued with him over it. Staple then hit Preston over the head with a bar stool, sending Preston to the hospital. According to some reports, Preston called Staple a nigger. But rather than explain the alleged racist comment to a judge, Staple chose not to show up for his court appearance and he never returned to Chicago since there was a warrant out for his arrest. Even though he continued to live in California for a number of years after the arrest, today, back in England, he has been denied a visa to the U.S. unless he goes to Chicago to settle the warrant. He chose not to return to the U.S. so any future reunion of the original lineup on U.S. tour will have to settle Staple's legal issues first. Staple, in his autobiography *Original Rude Boy*, sticks to an ambiguous story told in a *Rolling Stone* article rather than detail the events himself.

In late 2008, the Specials announced they would re-group for a 2009 30th anniversary tour, but Jerry Dammers said he would not be part of the plan. Byers explains,

> We tried working again with Jerry Dammers for two rehearsals but his ideas were weird even for him. He wanted to slow the old songs down and do new modern jazz versions live! Also he said we had to obey him completely, which he has since denied that he said this in the U.K. national press. The Reunion Tour was a strange experience for me and I think the rest of the band, with Jerry not being there and none of us realizing how much we meant to the old and new fans. We all kept pretty much to ourselves on tour as we always did whenever possible. I thought the music was played better and sounded more professional as we have all improved musically. It was very nice after each show chatting with the fans and hearing how much it meant to them. Very humbling really.

For ska, the 2Tone label gave another audience and another sound to the brassy off-beat foundation, breathing new life into ska's horns and roots. Jamaican pioneers saw a rebirth in their careers and they were shown respect with a new interpretation of their music as the 2Tone artists covered and sampled their work.

CHAPTER SEVEN

So Hot You're Cool: The Beat's Dave Wakeling and Ranking Roger

I N ENGLAND, 1979 WAS A YEAR of great upheaval, in the government, in day-to-day living, as well as in the music industry. The past decade had seen the likes of such arena rockers as T. Rex, Led Zeppelin, Jethro Tull, Queen, and Pink Floyd lead the way, bringing heavy sounds but joining together masses in appreciation of shared tastes. So too did England's citizens have shared tastes in their day-to-day living, for the essentials of a good life — hard work, food on the table, and love for one another. But the 1970s were at an end, and the heavy sounds of endless rock anthems, and the good times of working hard and sharing a pint with a mate down the road, were now at a brutal end.

It was the finish of camaraderie as Margaret Thatcher took office in May 1979, beginning a system of government akin to the one Ronald Reagan trickled down in America only one and a half years later. Capitalism was now nurtured by the Conservative-led government and neighbors became competitors, each vying for a piece of the pie that dwindled in size. Thatcher increased taxes, hitting manufacturing businesses hard, closing their doors and sending their workers out onto the streets. Unemployment rose to its highest level since the 1930s. Competition was now a matter of survival. It was every man for himself in every city, town, and shire in England.

Such was the climate the English Beat was born into — an environment of competition, greed, survival. And even though the band was a product of this milieu, the English Beat fought hard not to become a competitor, but a neighbor, and to bring back the love and unity there once was among those who worked hard and lived together.

Dave Wakeling, born on February 19, 1956, in Birmingham, England, grew up with a love for music. Music was a natural progression for Wakeling, even though he had a number of different unrelated jobs prior to his work with the English Beat, including stints as a firefighter, construction worker, and even hazardous work in a car battery plant. He began writing music and lyrics as a child, a skill that carried him to great fame years later. "It was a teenage thing and also I'd been an avid schoolboy poet. I found myself writing lots of rhyming couplets and stuff and I also liked singing a lot. I found myself singing all of the time. I would just sing to myself, anything. And I could do pretty good impersonations of my favorite singers. I could do a superb Robert Plant. And then I grew into being able to do a passable David Bowie and a pretty convincing Bryan Ferry, and a close-your-eyes-you-couldn't-tell-the-difference Van Morrison. And I just loved singing, you know. It made my soul feel good. It meant pressure off. That and the schoolboy poetry," Wakeling says.

Growing up in Birmingham, a largely industrial city known as the "workshop of the world," Wakeling was exposed to the sounds of talented natives. "One of the first groups I saw when I was 13 was Black Sabbath one week and Led Zeppelin the following week, and they were both local Midland bands. Black Sabbath was from Birmingham and Robert Plant and John Bonham were from Stourbridge just outside of Birmingham, so we thought of them as local heroes. Although the band had been formed with the two session guys in London, we thought of them as local boys, really. So it was Black Country Rock. Of course, David Bowie wrote a song about it, 'Black Country Rock,' because Black Country was industrial, sort of coal and metal working areas surrounding Birmingham and black is the sort of smoke," says Wakeling.

And so Birmingham natives, Wakeling and Andy Cox, begin their band, the English Beat. Dave Wakeling recalls,

> Me and Andy [Cox, born January 25, 1956], the guitarist, had gone to school together — well, further education college — it was like a college. Instead of your last two years of high school, you could go to a further

education college and you didn't have to wear a school uniform. And so we had been roommates and started playing guitars together and had the start of some songs going and we moved to the Isle of Wight in the mid–70s. We were building solar panels for his brother-in-law and he was a little ahead of his time, and we were getting it together in the country, although we didn't realize that. So we played our songs by the open fire. We'd actually gotten about three or four songs together and people started saying, "they're really quite good, you should get together and do something."

So the two boys from Birmingham set out to form a group. But life on the Isle of Wight was secluded, remote, and without a plethora of musicians to tap for band building. "Well first we joined a group that was looking for guitarists and singers in the Isle of Wight, but it turned out to be a Thin Lizzy cover band. So we played our songs, about four songs that ended up on the first Beat album, and the manager of the Thin Lizzy band was the singer's girlfriend, and all the time we were singing "Best Friend" and you could see her sitting in the bar there just shaking her head, like, "uh-oh, this is not going to work." So we didn't get to sing our own songs, but I got to do a pretty good "Whiskey In a Jar," Wakeling says.

Dave Wakeling, co-founder, guitarist, and vocalist for the Beat, performs in Chicago in 2009. Wakeling says it was the band's mission to create a "punky reggae party," while at the same time conveying a message of love and unity (photograph Heather Augustyn).

Both Wakeling and Cox knew the Thin Lizzy cover band would never foster their creativity and talent, so they began looking for a different outlet. "We did the cover band for a

111

couple of weeks and then we thought, 'This isn't going to work.' And I put an advert in a local Isle of Wight newspaper saying a bass player was wanted, 'Shake Some Action,' which was the name of a song by the Flamin' Groovies that was just a favorite song of mine. And we thought that anyone on the Isle of Wight who knew that title of that song must be okay. Only one person answered the advert and turned up in a lime green sweater with music notes on it, and it turned out to be the genius David Steele, the dark angel of the bass, who went on to play bass for the Fine Young Cannibals," says Wakeling.

David Steele was only 17 when he joined the band and felt that Cox's and Wakeling's musical tastes were too eclectic for his own punk tendencies. Still, he had a passion for music, although he did pursue a career as a psychiatrist for a while before the success of the band enabled him to leave his steady work behind. Soon after the band began rehearsing, Steele earned the nickname "Shuffle," a term used to describe his awkward lurching dance moves while playing bass guitar, given to him by the mother of the next band member to join, Everett Morton.

"The three of us (Wakeling, Cox, and Steele) started playing songs but we soon realized it wasn't the choice of many people to do it within the Isle of Wight, so we moved back to Birmingham and started working with Everett," says Wakeling. Everett Morton came to the band through a colleague of Steele and his work at the All Saints Mental Hospital in Birmingham. Steele became close friends with many of the Jamaican nurses at the hospital and when he discussed his band's need for a drummer, one of his fellow employees, a nurse named Paulette Sherly, suggested a friend of hers, Everett Morton. Morton was a bit older than the rest of the boys, and he had more experience. Plus, he had first-hand knowledge of reggae rhythms since he was born on the island of St. Kitts in the West Indies and moved to England in the mid–1960s. They practiced together and decided that Morton was in the band.

They came up with the name of their band by pulling out a reference book and channeling one of their favorite groups. "Dave Wakeling and Andy Cox, who were the nucleus of the Beat, they were both into the Clash," says Ranking Roger. "So if you look under 'clash' in the thesaurus, you will see 'beat,' right? Because to clash is to beat, isn't it?" he says. Wakeling says, "I still have my 1973 *Roget's Thesaurus*. In the music

section under 'discord' I found 'clash,' under 'harmony' I found 'beat'!"
And later, the Beat had to undergo an Americanization when a band in
America had the same name. "That was because of Paul Collins Beat in
America. There was another band called the Beat in America. They were
crap anyway. Because they had a very heavyweight management, we had
to change our name to the English Beat, under the condition that they
find a new name and they became Paul Collins Beat—the singer, his
name was Paul Collins. So we became the English Beat in America,
which is a shame in a way, because it would've been nice to have been
known as the Beat everywhere," Ranking Roger says.

Finding band mates had proven successful, but now, according to
Wakeling, the job was to find the perfect sound, or the perfect blend of
sounds.

We had these house parties in Birmingham and we would have two DJs,
one spinning reggae 12-inch slates and another DJ spinning punk 7-inch
singles, colored fluorescent vinyl. And we found that if you played all
reggae songs it would eventually become sort of ambient and people
would just be leaning against the wall, nodding their heads, and if you
played all punk songs, the place would go absolutely nuts for the first
hour and then everybody would go and lie down somewhere and have a
rest. But if you mixed it up, spinning a reggae dub, a couple of punk
singles and another couple of reggae songs, another punk single, you just
mixed it up, following the flow of it during the night, then the dance
floor stayed packed all night and the punk songs built everybody's
energy levels up and exhilarated them and the reggae songs made everybody groovier and sexier. We were sitting on the floor of the party and
we used to empty all of the furniture and carpet out of this big room
where we had the party and Andy said to me, "Well what if you could
get elements of both DJs into the same three minute pop song, what
would you have then?" It was like, "Ta-da!" You'd have a punky-reggae
light bulb going off. So it was trying to blend the rhythmic insistence of
reggae with that sort of chug-chug-chug along of the Velvet Underground, Iggy Pop and the Stooges, and then mixing that with the catchi-
ness of '60s English pop and Motown and the acerbic edge lyrically and
musically of punk.

I can't say really that I'm a ska artist. We come from what we thought
was the punky reggae revolution. Punky reggae party, as Bob Marley
sang. We wanted to blend the exhilaration of punk and the sensuality of

reggae together in the same three minute song and once we were in the process of doing that, we realized how similar some of our grooves were sounding to the ska of the soccer terraces in England in the late '60s and early '70s, which had been the first reggae we had heard really, that skinhead reggae, that skinhead ska at soccer games. So it was kind of ska by default. That wasn't the starting point. We sort of hit upon it by trying to blend punk and reggae together. So once we got to that point, we mixed in bits of all of our favorite music as well, looking for the perfect black rose, so we mixed in Motown, which was a big favorite of ours.

The band agreed on a sound. Now the difficulty was to master that sound. Wakeling recalls the process:

So we kept practicing and it wasn't easy to start with because we all had very different musical backgrounds and musical preferences, but every now and then, the beat would just lock on and it was like, "Wow!" and it'd be something we'd never heard before. It had got all the elements of our favorite music and was instantly infectious to anybody who'd heard it. But it took a little while. Eventually, Everett the drummer said, "Why don't we learn a song we all know and develop our groove together with that and then come back to one of those weird songs you keep trying to do, like that Mirror thing?" So we learned "Tears of a Clown" and we would play "Tears of a Clown" and then we'd play one of our songs and then we'd play "Tears of a Clown" again and we'd play one of our songs, so we'd kind of blend the various styles as everyone was hitting one at the same point, and eventually we got it.

The band was not ready to do something with what they had. So the four band mates got ready to get some experience under their belts and in March 1979 they began performing live. "We started these shows. David Steele said that one show was worth a thousand rehearsals because there wasn't the same room for pretension. So we started doing a Tuesday night residency at a club called the Mercat Cross. And a lot of the nightclubs in Birmingham at the time wouldn't let punks or Rastas in cause they thought they might be trouble and there was a pub called the Crown that anybody could go to and this guy at The Mercat Cross agreed there'd be no restrictions on punks and Rastas. So a group of people from the Crown, the Crown Punks as they were known, used to come to our Tuesday night show, and Ranking Roger was one of those," remembers Wakeling. Almost instantly, Ranking Roger was in the group.

Ranking Roger was born as Roger Charlery on February 21, 1961, in Birmingham, although his roots were West Indian and his upbringing included tutelage in music and the arts. He recalls:

My parents were big time into music. My father was a saxophone player in his younger age, but when he was in the West Indies he played saxophone, and my mother was a dancer. I remember when I was younger watching her and thinking "brilliant" and when I was about eight or nine she was really at her peak, I guess. Where we live in Birmingham, all the different types of music get molded together. There are Indians, there are blacks, there are Chinese, there are all sorts of people who live in the parts of Birmingham where I grew up, so it naturally came on to me, as well as the other members of The English Beat. Most of them came from multicultural areas anyway. My parents were from the West Indies and I was born in England. They were from a Caribbean island called St. Lucia, which is a French-speaking country. St. Lucia music is more calypso-oriented. They're still into the old African thing I guess, where ska really comes from Jamaica, and of all the West Indians in England, there is a bigger Jamaican population, so we were hearing a lot of Jamaican music. We got pulled into that as well and it became a part of our culture.

He drew upon his upbringing in the musical arts as a young teenager, beginning his own band, a punk outfit called the Dum Dum Boyz, named after the Iggy Pop song. Ranking Roger performed, not as a vocalist or toaster, but as a drummer. "We were together only about three to five months, but we did a few gigs and obviously I really always wanted to be a singer, but drumming I was good at because I was into rhythm. I've always been into drum and bass. And so I put drum up as the first thing, just to get a taste of what it would be all about and it was pretty exciting really, I mean there were dangers there. People were really out of their heads and didn't know what they were doing half the time, but really it was a lot of kids shouting out against the system that had tried to separate people and had tried to make people think one particular way," says Ranking Roger.

Ranking Roger's band, the Dum Dum Boyz, played a gig with the English Beat in support and a relationship between band members was forged. Ranking Roger became friends with Wakeling and their paths began to cross even more.

One day they were playing this gig and this is before I joined them because I was still with the Dum Dum Boyz [says Ranking Roger]. We were just finishing the Dum Dum Boyz and we were about to split up and I used to go to this local pub, the Mercat Cross, and the Beat were playing and there were five people there. And I went up to Dave and I said, "Do you want me to go out and get some people for ya?" and he said yes, and I came back and must have brought between 50 and 70 punks into the pub. I said, "There's this band man and they're called the Beat and they're alright," so they all came. I mean there were police cars going past us thinking we were going to cause trouble, but I just told everyone there was this gig on, because it wasn't very well advertised, and they came to this gig and made the difference. I mean there were so many people there they couldn't fit anymore in. Because of that gig, the Beat got a residency there. The guy sold so much drink behind the bar, he just welcomed us. That was really the first of it.

Wakeling remembers that same gig and Ranking Roger's critical charisma. "At the time he was pure punk in army fatigues, a torn up Union Jack wrapped around him. To start with, his main job was he doubled the audience with him and his friends and then he started jumping up during the instrumental sections and we only had the one microphone and he'd grab that, and he would start toasting and rapping on, you know, what had been going on in Birmingham that week or who was in the crowd and what they were wearing or just jocular stuff and sort of emceeing and DJing the night, and it went down very well and we did that for a few weeks," says Wakeling.

Ranking Roger says he had a reputation for toasting even prior to his days at the Mercat Cross. "Not only was I in a punk band as a drummer, but on weekends I would go around toasting in nightclubs, toasting about love and unity — that was always my main theme. The other thing was, they used to have these big concerts. They were big in those days. They used to hold about 2,000 people. And they were Rock Against Racism gigs, and all the proceeds went towards trying simple things to combat racism when it was really bad in the late '70s with the National Front and the British Movement, and they put punk and reggae bands on the same bill and they were the first people to do it," he says. Rock Against Racism began as a response to the racist climate in England at the time, as well as racist remarks made by Eric Clapton and David

Bowie in concert and in interviews. The campaign was the plan of organizers Roger Huddle and Red Saunders who brought a series of concerts and music festivals to English music fans. Bands such as the Clash, Steel Pulse, Generation X, and the Buzzcocks participated in the shows.

> So I used to go to a lot of their concerts and when reggae bands came on, or the punk bands, it didn't matter, at some point I'd just jump on the stage and pick up the mic and start toasting and the audience started going mad. After three or four times of doing this, it started to become this weird thing, you know? "Will Ranking Roger toast tonight? Or will he get up there before security gets to him?" and things like that, because I used to essentially crash the gig. I'd wait till I heard a tune I knew I could toast a lyric to and then I'd grab the mic and start talking love and unity lyrics and the audience would all go mad, so the band couldn't throw me off, security couldn't touch me. Obviously because the audience was cheering twice as loudly as they were before I came on, the bands were usually alright about it in the end. But the fact is I made my first name through that. It wasn't really through the Beat, because I had a name in Birmingham [says Ranking Roger].

And that name, along with the name of the Beat, was about to get much bigger. After their big gig at the Mercat Cross with loads of Ranking Roger's friends, word got out. Wakeling remembers,

> Jerry Dammers from the Specials came to our show on a Tuesday and said there's this group called the Selecter and we had heard about the Specials by then. I should backtrack. We had heard about the Specials and we'd been practicing and David Steele came in with a *Melody Maker* (one of Britain's top music journals at the time) opened up to the middle page spread, threw it on the floor and went, "Too late, somebody's beaten us to it," and we were like, "What?" "Yeah, a group called the Specials in Coventry," which is only about 17 miles down the road, "They're blending punk and reggae," and we said, "No! That's meant to be our secret," although the Clash had done it, hadn't they? And we were big fans of the Clash. But anyway, we carried on regardless and Jerry Dammers showed up at a show and said, "There's this group called the Selecter and they're playing a show on Thursday in Blackpool," which was about 100 miles north of Birmingham. "They're playing on Thursday night, would you like to open for them?" And we said, "Yeah, sure!" And we got our first gig outside of Birmingham opening for the Selecter and there were some more Specials there and they all said how

great we were, and they said that Madness and the Selecter were playing together at a pub in London on Saturday night and would we like to open for the pair of them, and we said, "Yeah, sure." So we went to London, which was about 100 miles south of Birmingham, on Saturday and we met more of the Specials and got to tour more with the Selecter and we got to meet Madness and they all said how fantastic we were and they asked us, "We have this record label, 2Tone, and would you like to make a single?" and we were like, "Yeah, sure!" And from Tuesday to Saturday, that was it. Our career was fixed really. We started in March or April doing our residency, and we made the single in about October, and it came out just before Christmas and it was number six Christmas week. We were on *Top of the Pops* and all our friends were jealous. We were in heaven really.

We did our version of "Tears of a Clown" because we had been doing all sorts of shows, sometimes punk shows, sometimes reggae shows, sometimes student union shows, sometimes factory Christmas party shows, god knows what, whatever we could get. Sometimes the punky shows would go down best, sometimes the reggae shows would go down best. But every night we'd go out, no matter who we'd be playing to, "Tears of a Clown" made the whole room go crazy. And we knew the single was coming out at Christmas time, so we thought, well that's what we should have as our first single. Also, Chrysalis wanted "Mirror in the Bathroom," but wouldn't let us have the song on our first album, so we gave them "Tears of a Clown" instead. It's a great party song, everybody likes the original and so we brought that one out and it just took the charts by storm.

In fact, the band knew the song would be such a holiday party hit that they fought with 2Tone and Chrysalis to make sure it would come out before Christmas. Dammers tried to convince the Beat to postpone their release of the single until after Christmas in an attempt to prolong the publicity that 2Tone bands were receiving from their recent tours and other releases. Chrysalis also tried to get the Beat to wait, but the Beat knew the tune would be a huge dance hit and pushed to release it anyway. Their instincts were correct. "'Tears of a Clown' was number six that Christmas and within nine months of the band forming up, and within six months of me joining them, we end up number six in the charts that Christmas. It was a brilliant Christmas present," says Ranking Roger.

Perhaps more critical to the band's success than the timing of their first single was the addition of another dimension to their sound. The band, true to Jamaican ska tradition, and like the Specials did as well, realized the importance of adding brass to their sound. Everett Morton was colleagues with a saxophone player named Lionel Martin, better known in musical circles as Saxa. After the band witnessed his performance at a pub in Handsworth called the Crompton, they convinced the saxophonist to join their ranks.

At the time Saxa joined The Beat, he was in his mid 50s, born in Kingston, Jamaica, in 1930. Saxa performed at an early age with such Jamaican pioneers as Prince Buster, Laurel Aitken, and Desmond Dekker and later in England with the Beatles. "I've never met anybody like him," says Ranking Roger. "Out of this world, totally. A brilliant fellow. As soon as he plays a note, he's got everybody in a trance. He's said some profound things. At first you start thinking, 'This guy is bloody mad,' but then when you're in bed alone at night and you're thinking about it, 'What did he mean by that?' and then all of a sudden you see there's a lot of truth in the things he said. So he's kind of a mystic man, I would say." One could easily argue that the inclusion of saxophone in English ska bands, like Saxa's contribution to the Beat, paved the way for saxophone use in the bands that followed, such as Romeo Void and Oingo Boingo, and may have led the way to the now-cliché sax solos of bands such as Duran Duran, Quarterstick, INXS, Roxy Music, Spandau Ballet, Wham!, and Wang Chung, to name a few.

After the success of "Tears of a Clown," everyone was clamoring for a chance to ride the coattails of the Beat's success, and more importantly, their potential. But the Beat was a smart group and they had seen their own colleagues, the Specials, go down a path much to their liking. "In England there's always this saying, 'Never follow fashion. Always do your own thing.' And it's a good thing, really. After 'Tears of a Clown' was a hit, 2Tone was like, 'Anything! We'll sign you up. We'll give you a proper record deal,' and that, but we wanted our own record label and we didn't want the 2Tone label. We just wanted our own label so we could have artistic control because we realized we were in a position where we had at least ten major record companies circling around us at our gigs, wanting to sign us up because we had a hit. And it had been found out that we weren't signing to 2Tone and that was a very exciting time," says Ranking Roger. "Everyone had limousines, throwing things out for you to try to impress you. Obviously it never got past me," he says.

He continues, "So we decided to go with Arista Records in England. A couple of labels, even Chrysalis, who dealt with 2Tone, said to us, 'We'll give you your own label and we'll give you more money,' but we signed with Arista for less money and more freedom," says Ranking Roger. That freedom came in the form of a "key man clause" that specified that the band could get out of the contract and leave Arista at any time if the Arista representative who signed the contract left Arista. "It was a brilliant deal for those days. We could've got probably a half million pounds, more if we really wanted to, but we would've lost a lot of freedom. We wouldn't have been able to have sung about, or done, a lot of the things we actually ended up doing. And so we went for that and Go Feet! was formed," he says.

Wakeling concurs, "We suddenly, by January, had every major record label desperate to sign us up and so instead of going for what was just the biggest offer, we went toward a label that would give us our own version of 2Tone, the ability to have some artistic control over our own music and also to be able to invite people to bring their singles on our own label. So we started the Go Feet! label." The Beat went to work right away, establishing their label as a creative entity. They enlisted the help of illustrator Hunt Emerson who lived around the corner from Wakeling in Handsworth. Emerson designed a logo for the Beat, channeling a photo of Prince Buster dancing with a girl in early Jamaica, and like 2Tone's Walt Jabsco, the Beat Girl too was a simple black and white illustration. The Go Feet! logo featured feet that were positioned like a dance instruction chart.

"The first album we brought out was, we got to re-release our favorite record of all time that was very difficult to get a hold of. People were having to buy scratched-up second-hand copies of *The Heart of the Congos* album and we had that remastered and re-released on Go Feet! so that all of our friends could get a clean copy of our favorite record, which is very stupid! But we got to meet Cedric Myton and he came to live in Birmingham for a while and sang on the Beat's second album. He sang on 'Doors of My Heart' for us, so we got our hero on one of our records," says Wakeling.

The Beat also released their own singles and albums on Go Feet! and they discovered other bands they felt had promise. Ranking Roger says,

> We just carried on having hits on that label. We also put out a couple of other bands on that label. The Mood Elevators who were a band from Birmingham, and we put out a tune of theirs called "Annapurna" which didn't do anything in the charts but we wanted that record label, not necessarily as a hit machine, but really we put them on there because we loved them and we liked their kind of music. It was pop music, but kind of sounding slightly Arabian or Eastern or something like that. Very interesting and weird. And then we also put out the Congos, which were a band from Jamaica. We put out one of their albums which was never released in England called *Heart of the Congos* and we put out two albums by Cedric himself on that label as well. We were always on the road and we really wanted the label for ourselves and our friends, but really so we could have the artistic freedom to deal with it the way we wanted. But we did manage to get other people out on the label, but we were, in a sense, a proper record company.

In February 1980, the Beat released their second single and their first single for their newly-formed Go Feet! label. The single was "Hands Off She's Mine," and "Twist and Crawl," a double A side due to opposing thoughts within the group. The song "Hands Off She's Mine" went to number six in the charts. Arista and the Beat agreed it was time to record their first album and so they made *I Just Can't Stop It* at Roundhouse Studios in London, the very first album ever recorded in a digital studio, since Roundhouse had just undergone an equipment overhaul. The album was a blend of the members' different musical styles and tastes, and with a group ranging in age from their teens to their fifties, from the West Indies to the Isle of Wight, the result was a rich tapestry of sound.

"The English Beat were not really ska," says Ranking Roger, as if to shock.

> The English Beat used ska influences. When I grew up we had Indian music, we had African music, we had West Indian music, we had pop music, we had rock 'n' roll, I mean it was all there. I can't think of anywhere where you probably would've had so many different choices of music to choose from, and we had it in Birmingham because we had the

community then. It's not anymore, but then it was. So everybody got influenced by everybody else's music. It really didn't matter who you were, it's how you used it, you know what I mean? The first album was pretty up tempo and everything and I could say that there's definitely ska influences in there, but there are reggae influences in there too, and punk influences, and disco. There's everything in there, not just ska.

They released the single "Mirror In the Bathroom" as their second single on Go Feet! from their album in April 1980 and filmed their first video. After all, it was the start of the newly emerging MTV era. They filmed the video at a local pub called The Rum Runner. It was a start of a side of the music business that was in conflict with many of the members' philosophies. Wakeling says:

Some groups I think they got a video before they'd ever done a concert, which was really anathema to our post-punk sensibilities. Then we ended up doing videos ourselves though. I didn't like them very much ever because the parrot that was MTV had a long list of things that were verboten, like a list of 30 things that you couldn't have in a video, unless you were Madonna, then you had to have all 30 of them. It ended up you couldn't actually make a video that was about anything that was real or anything to do with right, honest sexuality. That was completely out, but all sorts of sexual stereotyping, that was perfectly fine. You could demean with it, that was fine. Have louvre blind windows opening and closing and a light swinging around while she writhes on a bed with a suitcase, that was fine, you could have that. But any display of honest sexuality was completely inappropriate.

But the exposure worked and their new album went straight to number three in the charts. Hit songs from *I Just Can't Stop It* include "Mirror In the Bathroom," "Hands Off She's Mine," "Best Friend," "Twist and Crawl, a very political tune called "Stand Down Margaret," and a cover of Prince Buster's "Rough Rider." The Beat's second album, *Wha'ppen*, was recorded at the same studio in June 1981, but in half the time and for half as much money as the first album, since digital recording was expensive and they were under pressure from Arista. These songs featured a slower ska tempo and were greatly influenced by the members' growing selection of African records as well as African instruments and Chinese instruments. The title of the album came after a considerable amount of brainstorming, producing such ideas as "Dance Yourself Stupid" and "Misdemean," among others. The band decided on the name *Wha'ppen?* which is a Jamaican term that Ranking Roger used to say to the band to ask them "What's going on?" very akin to Cluet Johnson's phrase in 1960s Jamaica, "Wha'up Skavoovie?," a term that may have coined the name ska.

Wha'ppen? saw the addition of another member to the lineup. Dave Wright, known as Blockhead, tickled the ivories as the Beat's guest keyboardist. Blockhead was 38 when he joined the group and had years of experience, performing most notably with the British group XTC and also in a steel band in St. Kitts called the Casanovas. Blockhead, like many of the other members of the Beat, held many other jobs before becoming a full-time musician, including working as a geography teacher and a social worker. As a long-time resident of Birmingham, Blockhead played piano at the local pubs before pursuing his dream.

Wha'ppen? was released in June 1981 and featured the hit songs "Doors of Your Heart" and "Too Nice to Talk To," but the album didn't do as well in the charts as their debut album. The band, realizing the 2Tone bubble had burst in England, began to look for another way to capitalize on their success. They looked to their U.S. market and rebranded themselves under a new U.S. label, I.R.S. Records, whose new wave image recorded bands such as REM and the Go-Gos. I.R.S. rereleased the English Beat's first two albums in the U.S. and produced the English Beat's third and final album, *Special Beat Service* in 1982. Hits included the classic "Save It For Later" and "I Confess," both of which received heavy airplay on MTV.

Why then did the Beat call it quits shortly after the release of this album, especially with such success in both the U.S. and England? The main reason was the exhaustive touring, the same nail in the Specials' coffin. "We broke up because of a lot of things. All of the tiredness was one, because we had done so many tours, especially in America," says Ranking Roger. The Beat also found the U.S. was in conflict with their musical aspirations and personal philosophies, while others thought the U.S. was an acquired taste. The constant touring in the U.S. nonetheless put stress on the group. Ranking Roger recalls, "The thing with the Beat is, the first time we came to America, that was something else. It was 1981 I think and we came over with the Pretenders. We opened up for them and did some gigs with the Talking Heads as well, that was quite good. Oh yeah. And that was our first introduction to America. It was a surprise to see how many seats there were and people eating hamburgers while they were watching the band. That was the American way of doing things. I just wasn't used to the American way of doing things. After the tenth time I came to America I can fit right in now. At first it was very strange," he says.

Wakeling says the internal dynamics of the group were always good, but the touring was hard and so direction on where to take the band differed from member to member.

> It was an experiment in the first place, a synthesis of styles. It wasn't like a peer group. We hadn't all gone to school together. Roger was 16 when the group started and Saxa was in his mid 50s and we all had different backgrounds and preferences, so we didn't really have any peer group arguments because we kind of expected that everyone would think totally different from everyone, and whilst everybody was infused with all those various ideas into a melting pot, we got to the heart of the matter. But then a combination of people developing separate ambitions and also some of us really like working live and some people really didn't like touring at all. They hated playing the same song over and over again and hated being on the road and eating crappy food and talking with drunk people for hours afterward, so that became a strain.

Plus, the Beat's popularity began to wane when 2Tone was falling out of fashion. "Our popularity started to get big in America and at the same time it started going down in England because we were taking too long to bring the next album out, like two years to bring the next album out instead of six months and that was because we had been spending like 18 months in America," says Ranking Roger.

Wakeling agrees:

> Like a lot of fashion waves in England, the quicker you go up, the quicker you're going to come down, and three years later 2Tone wasn't the flavor of the month, by definition, and the New Romantics (Depeche Mode, Spandau Ballet, Adam & the Ants, Culture Club, Duran Duran, etc.) had sashayed their way into town and it suddenly now looked a bit

old fashioned to be wearing street clothes and singing about unemployment. All of a sudden you needed to be wearing your mom's clothes and singing about yachts in the Caribbean. It goes to show you that music has a number of different functions. You can use it as a form of protest but also sometimes people need to use music as a form of pure escapism, and both parts of it are valid I think. So the combination of a diminishing sense of being pop stars in England at the time and to some of the band, even more scary was the fact that we were becoming huge rock stars in America. And that they hated even more, some of them. We were just becoming an American stadium rock act. It was like, "Well we had 20,000 people last night so we were great," and they were like, "Yes, exactly, it was horrible." And that caused some problems. And some of the band felt that people worked too hard and the phrase that sticks in my mind is, "Well there are more planes than busses now these days," and there was this fear that we'd become part of the rock world and singing songs about being on a tour bus and losing connection with where we'd come from and why we'd written songs in the first place.

And those songs were important. The band realized the value of the genre of ska as a way to bring about change and expound upon a social condition. Songs like "Stand Down Margaret" and "Get a Job" resonated with listeners who were facing issues of unemployment, racism, and violence. "Stand Down Margaret" pointed the finger at the source. Lyrics included the following lines:

> You tell me how can it work
> in this all white law
> what a short sharp lesson,
> what a third world war
>
> I sometimes wonder
> if I'll ever get the chance
> just to sit with my children
> in a holiday jam
> our lives seem petty in your cold grey hands
> would you give a second thought
> would you ever give a damn, I doubt it
> stand down Margaret
> Awoah!

> Everybody shout it
> stand down Margaret!

"Get a Job" detailed the dire situation that had become a reality for listeners:

> There's a training course
> boys and girls of real ambition
> start a new job in a factory
> where they're making ammunition
> but it makes them think of stealing
> when they read between the lines
> through the owners of this funfair
> you won't find a ride you like
> just get-a-job, get-a-job
>
> manufacture rubbish
> although no one can afford it
> you could make a profit
> more than anyone deserves
> so you find you're left with poison
> so you dump it in our water
> and so create the kind of problems
> only radiation cures
> through get-a-job, get-a-job
>
> oh you young people are revolting
> 8 to 5 should give the jolt needed
> in a few years you won't feel quite the same
> you'll be playing their get-a-job games
>
> there's a training camp when
> you come home from saving nations
> get a new job and a new leg
> social rehabilitation
> every time you think of leaving
> you get caught between the lines
> it's the training for the funfair
> you get taken for a ride

YOU!
get-a-job, get-a-job
just get-a-job, get-a-job

And like the tradition founded by the Jamaicans decades earlier, the content of the song was describing the social situation, while the tempo and the tone of the music was upbeat and a relief to the listeners. "You can sing in an uplifting beat about situations of social deprivation. Although life is tragic, it's still beautiful, and if you contemplate on that part of it, the tragedy doesn't disappear, but it becomes easier to bear," says Wakeling.

The composition of the Beat too was a social comment on unity and diversity. "If anybody had consciously tried to set it up as a social answer to the right wing extremism that was coming up out of the frustration about unemployment, I think if anyone had consciously said, 'I know, let's get a group of different colored people and sing about love and unity,' I think it perhaps wouldn't have worked. These things evolve out of the fabric of society, out of genuine concern for the frustration of the way that you could see people using the situation for their own personal gain. And it just ended up hitting a note that I don't think it could have hit if you sat and tried to plan it out," Wakeling says.

Ranking Roger says that the love and unity the band stood for may have been affected or tainted by the lure of fame and fortune, tearing the group apart and sending everyone their separate ways to pursue other opportunities.

There was a bit of confusion there toward the end. And a lot of confusion from Dave Wakeling to me because he really talked me out of leaving the Beat in reality. I know I left on my own accord, but he spent six months, because we used to share a hotel room together, and he spent the last six months of the Beat, you know, showing me all of these figures. So I would pull it down to the Beat split up because of greed, because me and Dave realized that if we went off and formed another band we would be earning two or three times as much than if we did this. Already everyone was asking for Dave and Roger. And I think it got to his head more than mine. But it must have got to both of our heads because we made that move. But I do say that three times before he said that he was going to leave and if I wanted to come with him I could and I said no, I'm not interested because this is the best thing I've ever had happen in my life and it's so true. The democracy of the Beat was so perfect. I've never known another band to have a democracy so fair like ours was, and I am partly to blame for destroying that democracy. In a way, I probably paid my price wanting to be greedy and so is Wakeling.

Wakeling says the end of the Beat and the start of their new band, General Public, was just a natural progression of the work Wakeling and Ranking Roger had been doing with the Beat. "Me and Roger like touring very much anyway. In some ways we preferred the moment of singing on stage to the endless singing something over and over again in the studio. We had some songs that had been brewing but we'd never managed to get together. The whole thing seemed magical and charmed the way it was set up, and we promised each other, well me and Andy had, once the magic started to disappear, we'd knock it on the head straight away. Too many acts seem to just carry on because that's what they did, regardless of whether the music was relevant, and so we knocked it on the head," says Wakeling. "I followed my musical nose, but Roger seems more influenced by the money," he says.

Wakeling contends it was a matter of meeting the group's needs:

Some of the band wanted two years off and me and Roger had just started families, although we probably could have fancied two years off, but even still, we couldn't afford two years off. The Beat hadn't been a socialist commune, but we'd share everything equally in terms of the song writing and the royalties and all that, so nobody had made a great deal of money and certainly not enough to have two years off and with new families. So we carried on and made General Public. We didn't really have much of a break. I left the Beat on Independence Day, it was '83 or '84, one of those, and we had a record out the next year, then went back to touring and promoting our record. [That record, *All The Rage* was a success, especially in the U.S.] It ended up being a pretty big hit, with the hit single "Tenderness" and "Never You Done That" and "Hot You're Cool" which was number one in the dance charts and number one in the year's chart for *Billboard*, which was really cool. I bought extra copies and clipped it out because General Public was number one and number two was Madonna. I stuck it in a Christmas card for my mom and dad.

Ranking Roger says that he enjoyed working with Wakeling in General Public, but as the lineup changed, so too did his feelings about the band.

> General Public did quite well at first but by the time we got to our second album we totally changed the band around, so there was only me and Dave and the bass player from the original General Public setup and basically we kept doing that, and really I don't think that way you can build a band if you keep — see General Public was meant to be me and Dave in the beginning and really all of the other musicians were meant to be used and dumped as we needed them, which is probably a crude way of me putting it across. And I think because of that there's no way it could've ever been a band like the Beat or a band that survives because really there was no time to get used to the organics of making music — the combination of the guitar to the bass and how they play with each other every night, and the drum to the vocal, stuff like that, where you get a mold. I mean the Beat, we got used to a mold, where no matter how tired, we could just go on and produce that sound automatically and that was from years of hanging out together, not changing round, you know?

General Public brought together two former members of Dexy's Midnight Runners, drummer Andy "Stoker" Growcott and keyboardist Mickey Billingham. Horace Panter, former bassist for the Specials, Saxa, and guitarist Mick Jones from the Clash all performed for the first album, *All the Rage*, released by I.R.S. in 1984. The album produced the song "Tenderness" that was a top 40 hit in the U.S. and a top 60 hit in England and used in the 1985 movie *Weird Science*. The video for the song was different in the U.S. than it was in England. Wakeling recalls the U.S. version:

> It was me and Roger as little kids. There were two little kids that were meant to look like us. The first video that we'd made in England was absolutely banned here in America. It was meant to be ambiguous. We got this great young director who had done the Bronski Beat video so we ended up, well I fall in love with a female body builder in a swimming pool and we ended up entwined around each other and then she rips her wig off and has this crew cut and I'm suddenly ensnared in these massive arms. We showed it to the American record company and they were like, "Oh, yes, that's very good. Okay, now here's a list of directors," [laughs].

The main thing then was to have lots of shots of my eyes and they put some drops in them to make the blue look even bluer and it seemed to work very well. My mom said, "Oh your eyes look lovely in that video." So it worked I suppose. What you were meant to remember was Roger's hair and Dave's blue eyes. Miles Copeland who was I.R.S. Records and managed the Police at the time gave everybody, and gave us as well, this pep talk. He said, "Don't for a minute start believing that you're selling music." We were like, "What?" He said, "No, no, you're not selling music, you're selling sex and if they find you sexy they'll listen to your songs." I said, "Well, thanks."

Their next album, *Hand to Mouth*, released in 1986, had significant lineup changes. The band split up soon after and Wakeling and Ranking Roger went their separate ways. Wakeling moved to Los Angeles in 1987, drawn by the sunshine as opposed to the dreary Birmingham clouds. He says that he and Ranking Roger just grew apart musically.

Roger had a growing feeling he wanted to do solo stuff and he became enamored with machinery that you can make music with now, whereas I was still a bit of a primitive. I liked an acoustic guitar and spend a few weeks writing something and then play it to a room full of people. Roger liked to build things one note at a time with the machines, and so our song writing styles began to diverge. When we started off in General Public, Roger would come up with really catchy instrumentals and I would start a line of lyrics going and he'd add to it and then I'd add to it, and we'd build on top of that, say like in "Never You Done That." But after the first General Public record, Roger wanted to do whole songs where he'd done all the music, all the lyrics and the lead vocal and he didn't want to do toasting, he wanted to be a singer and it ended up really that the songs were starting to sound like the Beatles when you used to get the John Lennon side and the Paul McCartney side. It was on the same record. And it was frustrating because we weren't getting the best out of each other which had been our collaborations, playing off of the different styles, and so that kind of fizzled out and I decided to move to California.

Although they did come back together as General Public in 1994 to record the Staple Singers' cover song "I'll Take You There" for the soundtrack for the movie "Threesome," and again in 1995 for an album, *Rub It Better*, Wakeling and Ranking Roger had a strained relationship over the years. Wakeling says it has been hard to put his finger on:

We had a bit of an iffy period but made a very warming and reassuring truce. We'd been trying to get back together to do something. Oddly though, some of the people who were surrounding us, they would kind of stick hurdles up in the way. I think there was a genuine interest from me and Roger to do something, but Roger is working as the Beat in England and he has a whole band and organization around him, and certain people in that center didn't want Roger and me working together. They felt they might be on the outs if we did. So there's been some general reluctance in people who worked around both of us who kind of made it more difficult. It doesn't look like it's going to happen and we're 6,000 miles apart. It's not like you can just pop in for a week-end, so we decided we had tried to work together and it didn't look like it was going to happen in the near future, so instead of carping about it, we'd just wish each other the best of luck and get on with it. Be friends from a distance instead of close enemies, and we were both relieved by that. We also, whatever our differences might be about, had to go about things and we realized that we were very lucky to have been together and when we got to make some music, it really moved people, and it became embarrassing that we were singing about love and unity on different sides of the Atlantic, but we couldn't talk to each other, and it was embarrassing that the love and unity guys couldn't be love and unity to each other [laughs].

So we had to confront that and we made our peace and in some ways, by both of us being a bit competitive with each other the last couple of years, it's forced both of us to really work hard on our careers and so I know, I suppose again by accident, you've got a group called the Beat doing a tour of quite prestigious venues, and you've got a band called the English Beat playing a list of really knock-out venues here in America, so the Beat will be playing two shows in two different venues on the same weekend. So it's kind of worked out for the best, by not being as friendly as we might have been, that bit of competition I think pushed both of us to really get our act together. So there are actually two quite powerful bands. Of course mine's better. Roger would probably laugh if he hears this one. We realized that we learned a great deal from each other and the few times we have performed together over the last few years it immediately clicked. We'd come on stage and people would go, "The magic's still there." We'd be looking at each other and be singing the songs and either by accident or just by muscle memory, we'd do some dance move that we used to do together fifteen or twenty years ago. God, we still knew that. And so there's a lot of history and so I'm relieved that although we're not likely to work together in the near future, we've left the door open, that who knows whatever might happen in the future, and at this point we just wish each other all the very best of luck and we can more comfortably spread the message of love and unity to two or three continents now.

Andy Cox and David Steele, meanwhile, established a group of their own, Fine Young Cannibals, named after the 1960 Natalie Wood and Robert Wagner movie by the same name. They released two albums, a self-titled debut album in 1985 and *The Raw and the Cooked* in 1989. Neither album continued the tradition of ska or any ska influence of note, although they did spawn several dance hits, including "She Drives Me Crazy" and "Good Thing." They broke up in 1992 and reunited again in 1996 to record a single before again dissolving.

Dave Wakeling worked full time for Greenpeace for five years, taking on special projects and executive producing an album for Greenpeace called *Alternative NRG*. This album was recorded in 14 different venues and studio trucks that used solar power. Among those on the album were REM, UB40, Sonic Youth, U2, and Midnight Oil. Wakeling recorded a solo album, *No Warning*, and he continues to tour with the English Beat, comprised of himself and other new members, although the sound is still the same as he plays all of their old hits. In 2003, he joined the other original members of the Beat, minus Andy Cox, for a small reunion tour of England. In 2006, the Rock and Roll Hall of Fame asked Wakeling to donate his trademark Vox teardrop guitar for an exhibit, alongside other guitars from such greats as Kurt Cobain and Jimi Hendrix. The Vox teardrop guitar he uses on stage today is a copy of his original. Wakeling brought sold-out audiences 150 shows in 2009 in the U.S. as the English Beat, performing 17 new songs, and was recording in 2010. "The Beat lives on!" he says.

Ranking Roger had a solo career for years after General Public broke up. He says:

Me and Dave, we stopped working with the General Public thing and he went to live in America and I stayed in England and within about a year I had put out my album *Radical Departure*. The lyrics from that album were really profound, but very true to the way I felt at the time. I had a lot of anger in me and I had a lot of things to say that were actually negative with a ray of hope. Well I should say they were a lot of warnings to people, not to say that I thought I was some prophetic person, it wasn't like that. It was more things that I saw that I just didn't think people looked into deep enough, you know? And so that album proved to be far too political. I think it sold somewhere between seventy and one hundred thousand. In English terms that would be seen as, "Well done, lad, pat on the back."

That album produced one popular song and video for the song "So Excited." In 2001, he released a second solo album called *Inside My Head*. Both albums were greatly influenced by ska, reggae, and dub, along with other genres such as pop and dance. For Ranking Roger, the music is all a blend stemming from rhythm and blues. "The roots of reggae music, the roots of ska music, even the roots of pop music, I mean they all come from rhythm and blues. In a way, all the music we listen to that's 4/4 timing, if you like, that we accept as popular music today, all comes from rhythm and blues. That's really the roots of it, so reggae is just part of the family really, and ska is just a part of the family, so soul and jazz, they all come from the same roots at the end of the day," he says.

Ranking Roger also toured with a blended band consisting of members from other ska bands. "I went out and tried Special Beat, which was half the Beat and half the Specials, or it was supposed to have been. I was the only member representing the English Beat, but we survived for about four years," says Ranking Roger. In that four years, the Special Beat toured with Steel Pulse and Sting. "It was a very energetic show, you see. We used to kill the audience. They just wanted more all the time. We used to come off like the River Jordan, always drenched. I could always ring my T-shirt easily and that's when we knew we'd done a good show. So that was brilliant, but that came to an end. Obviously we weren't going to sign any record deal and we just wanted to be a live band and there weren't really any new numbers, so we kind of fizzled out," he says. Yet the band did produce three live albums, two in 1994 and one in 1998, as well as an album of the new band covering their old hits called *Gangsters* also in 1998. The group has toured periodically over the years.

Another incarnation of the original band emerged as International Beat, and there was also a British Beat. Ranking Roger explains:

In Australia we were known as the British Beat. The International Beat were not the Beat. Actually it was the International Beat who inspired me to form the Special Beat. The International Beat was the original drummer from the Beat and Saxa, the original saxophonist from the Beat, and they were the only two members of the English Beat who were in there and then there was this guy who called himself Tony Beat for some reason, because he's beat mad, and he thinks he's Dave Wakeling, right? And there was also this black guy called Louie who thought he was me. So as far as I'm concerned, they were trying to be the English Beat again, but what ever happened with them? It turned out I ended up producing their album and because, well I produced half of it and this guy Mickey Billingham who was in General Public, our keyboard player, he produced the other half, and that was really difficult because I ended up saying to one of them, "Try singing this," and then they wouldn't be able to do it so I'd have to go out there myself and do it. It was terrible actually, to tell the truth. Their album, what they came out with, I think Mickey and I did a great job in getting that. I think they rushed it, the budget wasn't enough, and it was done really unprofessionally.

Through it all, the Beat were a slice of life at the time — a mouthpiece for the social issues facing English youth, and a representation of the love and unity they preached. And even if that proved difficult over the years, after all, that was reality, that relationships can be hard. And it is only in hindsight, with the microscope of analysis that we can see now the snapshot of what once was.

When the Beat started with three white guys and three black guys, we didn't know there was anything special about it, to be honest, until we went to London and played our first gig there and everybody was talking about it like it was a sociology experiment [says Wakeling]. And they like it, but we were three white geezers and three black geezers on stage together, and by the time we brought the band to New York, then it really had become a sociology thing. People thought we had put the group together like marketing research or a Benetton ad. And then, of course, we accepted it. As long as they thought it was a good idea we didn't care why they thought it was a good idea, but it hadn't really seemed anything that out of the ordinary coming from this industrial and then post-industrial melting pot.

Wakeling says the function of their music, and the function of ska was vital during the late '70s and early '80s. He compares this function to modern times as well as to Jamaica in the '60s and '70s.

There was the fear of recession, the spector of nuclear exchange, the sort of smell of war in the air and a little bit of a lack of social direction about how people are going to actually confront some of the obvious ills that face the human race and it's kind of like people are looking for a music that gives people the ability to protest, but at the same time also allows you to pick your own spirits up. It's like you don't want to be angry or nihilistic like they might have had during the punk times and in the '90s grunge times, things are a bit too serious for that, so you want to be able to comment and protest, but in an uplifting way because you want to pick your own life up, your own spirit up, and I think that's one of the pieces that I got early on from reggae was that, you would hear this beautiful song and you'd feel all happy and cheery and then you'd get drawn into the lyrics of the song and you'd see so often that people were singing about oppression or deprivation. If you listen, say, to Max Romeo's "Uptown Babies," and what a pretty song, [sings] "Uptown babies don't cry," and then you realize, "Oh my god, he's singing about starving children in the ghetto," but you don't notice that to start with because of the uplifting feel to it, and I think that's been one of the pleasures and the gifts of working in this style of music.

Ranking Roger says the impact of their band and the impact of others during their era was critical:

In a way, we did actually change history. I mean if it wasn't for punk, then ska the second time man, when the Specials and the Beat and Madness and all them bands came about, they would never have stood a chance because we came out of punk. The punks were sayin' the same things that we were sayin', it was just probably a bit more slightly mellow because we came up the back of new wave. People could accept it all of a sudden because for the first time the Jamaican influences got accepted in British society and culture because of the things we were saying. And when ska came out in the '60s, it was a big social thing but it was very underground. This time around it became more commercial. It's forever growing.

Despite the social messages the Beat were conveying, the competition that had seeped into Thatcher-led England in the early 1980s, and the MTV-era-sex-sells-not-music-have-a-seat-at-the-concert-and-eat-a-cheeseburger America became the downfall of the band. The constant touring, especially in America where many of the band members had an adverse reaction to capitalistic culture, and the competition from within despite the organic democracy that once made the group a family, became the eventual demise of the band that stood for love and unity. Now those band members pass that message along, perhaps now a bit wiser, to their own audiences in their own way.

CHAPTER EIGHT

More Than a "Three Minute Hero": The Selecter's Pauline Black with Millie Small

FOR SOME ARTISTS, their craft is not learned; it's part of their being from day one. For the Selecter's Pauline Black, music was a part of her nature, rather than a nurtured skill. Quite simply, music was in Pauline Black's blood, and that innate ability allowed her band to have success while it existed, as well as leaving an indelible fingerprint on music as a whole.

Pauline Black was born Pauline Vickers on October 23, 1953, in Romford, Essex, England. "At that time, I didn't know who my real family was because I was adopted at an early age. My adoptive family was white," says Black. "My birth mother was Jewish and my birth father was Nigerian. It's an interesting combination. I finally met my birth mother in 1996 and discovered that I've got a half brother, who was a bass player in a band in Australia. He had some success in the Sydney area and released CD's and toured in the early eighties. It's amazing to think that neither of us knew anything about each other until 1996. My Nigerian grandfather played piano very well too. My mother sings. She's got a very good voice. My musical genes were there, but I didn't know about them. Nobody was musical in my adoptive family," she says.

Black says she found interest in the artists that were popular in East London where she grew up, despite the fact that her neighborhood was

Pauline Black, vocalist for the Selecter, photographed in 1980, brought her moxy and gift to a male-dominated industry. Black says her early influences included Millie Small and Desmond Dekker (photograph courtesy Pauline Black).

not ethnically or racially diverse. The music she heard had a big impact on the music she soon would create of her own. "The people whose music I like the most were the obvious, Millie Small, 'My Boy Lollipop,' and Desmond Dekker. I had never heard anybody, one, with a voice like Millie Small, and two, that kind of music. I grew up in a white neighborhood and my adoptive parents didn't listen to that kind of music so I used to access music either through school friends who might have records, and they were pretty few and far between at that particular age and that time, or through the radio. I heard Millie Small's 'My Boy Lollipop' first on the radio, same as Desmond Dekker's 'Israelites,'" says Black.

Millie Small was born in Clarendon, Jamaica, on October 6, 1946. Her full name was Millicent Small and she began singing at a very young age. Small remembers, "It just happen naturally for me. I was born to be a singer and I have no family history of musical knowledge. I'm the first and last in the family to become a recording artist. My break came when I was 12 years old. I entered the Vere Johns talent show and won and from there on everyone wanted to record with me including Roy, and we done some really good songs together." Roy Panton was Small's singing partner. The duo recorded for Clement "Coxsone" Dodd at Studio One. "Those days were really fun days and people are still playing those songs at home, parties, and in the car. Those songs we did together will live forever it seems," says Small. Those songs included such hits as "We'll Meet," "You're the Only One," "Oh Merna," and "Marie." She also recorded duos with Owen Gray and Jackie Edwards.

After hearing Small perform at the Ward Theatre in Jamaica, Robert Blackwell, Chris Blackwell's brother who was also in A&R for Island Records, liked Small's voice and contacted her to record for their label. He brought her to England in late 1963 where she produced her classic hit, "My Boy Lollipop" that went on to sell seven million copies. The song was a cover song of the 1956 American R&B song recorded by Barbie Gaye that had no real success. Small was backed by Jamaican guitar great Ernest Ranglin who arranged the tune, and harmonica was performed (contrary to rumor that claims a young Rod Stewart had the role) by Pete Hogman of the Pete Hogman Blues Band and Hoggie & the Sharpetones. Small recalls, "When Chris Blackwell gave me the tune to learn at first I did not like it but I grow to like it the more I sang it over and over again. Also, I did not feel anyway in particular about it when I actually recorded it, I just went with the flow and did the best I could and as a result it got to number two in both the U.K. and U.S. charts in 1964." In fact, the song sold over seven million copies internationally.

The impact of "My Boy Lollipop" on the ska world was huge. Continuing in a new market, England, the ska sound was now a pleasant pop surprise, fresh and light like the singer herself. And the impact on female musicians, like Pauline Black, was also significant since Small had now cleared the path for future successes. Small says, "I was young so I did not think about the impact at the time of 'My Boy Lollipop's' success but it took me to many parts of the world and I also met many stars and interesting people everywhere I go. One thing for sure, it open the door for all Jamaican artists, male or female, that follows thereafter up to this point. Also, it was the first ska disc to make it globally and the influence it carries still exists and is evident today. All in all, this disc is the only ska recording I'm told that sold over seven million copies to date, of which no other female Jamaican artist has surpassed yet."

For Black, Small, as well as Desmond Dekker, was a big musical influence as a child. "Both of them I feel had quite an impact on how I felt about Jamaican music. Because it was so fresh. I really really enjoyed it. At least another 15 years would go by before I would try and do it. It was just something you enjoyed, you danced to, you talked about, and I guess as well that the particular school I went to had quite a high proportion of young people who thought that the skinhead culture was really good and so they'd adapt the school uniforms to look very skinhead. They'd bring 'Long Shot Kick De Bucket' and other songs by the Pioneers, stuff by Toots and the Maytals, but I was the only black kid at my school so I became aware that there was a whole load of white kids who were listening to black music and they didn't understand why I didn't know about it," she says.

Still, despite Black's love for Jamaican music, she decided to pursue a career not in music, but in medicine. "My background had been in science. I came to Coventry to go to university and I was doing a degree in biochemistry and kind of choked on that. After about two years I thought, 'I need to move on.' So I became a radiographer, which I think in America is an x-ray technician and I worked at a local hospital here in Coventry and sang and played guitar with local musicians in the evening," Black says.

Her singing began at local clubs and grew through her affiliations with other musicians, eventually leading her to the other members of the Selecter. "I first started off, just myself and a guitar playing in clubs, because that's the only place where you can play and nobody takes too much notice when you drop any bum notes. So I started doing that when I was about 22. I got to know a few musicians who thought that it would be a good idea to write together and from that I got to know some other people who were around the reggae scene in Coventry and some of those people would then go on to be in the Selecter. Some of them were already in a local reggae band called Hard Top 22. Charles "Aitch" Bembridge and Desmond Brown worked with me in a band that I was getting together. We played songs I had written that were reggae-ish in flavor. One day, Lynval Golding from the Specials turned up at a rehearsal and sort of cherry picked me and 'H' and Desmond and said, 'I think you should go and meet some guys I know who are trying to put a band together,' and what he meant was go meet Neol Davies and the rest of the Selecter basically," she says.

Neol Davies (pronounced Neil) was born in 1952. He was inspired at an early age by such musicians and bands as the Who, the Beatles, Duane Eddy, and the Shadows. But it wasn't until he attended a concert at the Coventry Theatre and saw first-hand the genius of Jimi Hendrix that Davies decided to make the guitar his instrument. Like many of the other members of the Selecter and the Specials, Davies moved in musician circles in Coventry and got to know many of the original members of these bands by performing with them in their many pre–2Tone incarnations. Among those bands for Davies were Chapter 5 and Night Train. Davies became friends with Lynval Golding of the Specials during these formative years. Along with John Bradbury, who was soon to join the Specials, Davies composed and recorded an instrumental in his garden shed in the summer of 1977 and the tape sat until early 1979 when it resurfaced as a B side called "The Selecter," a song whose name inspired the name of the band to come. The A side of that single was "Gangsters," by the Specials. When Jerry Dammers recorded and pressed "Gangsters," he borrowed money from a friend to fund the effort. Only later did Dammers realize he left no money for the flip side, so Lynval Golding called his friend, Neol Davies, and offered him the opportunity to release his song. Dammers also invited Bradbury to perform drums for "Gangsters," since the Specials' drummer, Silverton Hutchinson, had just quit. Bradbury continued on in that capacity. Davies was now involved in the birth of not only the Specials, but the birth of the Selecter and the birth of 2Tone.

Because Davies saw the creation of 2Tone to be an exclusive and timely opportunity, he was brought into the negotiations between the Specials and Chrysalis, and because Davies was a colleague of the members of the Specials, Davies quickly formed a band, named after his B-side tune, the members of which became, along with the members of the Specials, directors of 2Tone. "We became joint directors of the 2Tone label. We could sign bands of our choice to the label," says Black. All 14 of the members of the two bands were to have an equal share in the label, but as the months went on, Davies, Black, and the other members of the Selecter would soon see they really had no input at all.

The band was officially formed in June 1979 by Davies who pulled together Black (who had changed her name from Vickers to suit her entertainment persona, especially in case she decided to return to the medical field) and the others for an initial meeting to introduce the new sound. "We all met up one night. We listened to Neol's track, 'The Selecter,' which was an instrumental track and that ended up on the B side of the Specials' 'Gangsters,' which was their first single release in this country. We were very impressed that Neol got on a record with one of his songs. And it transpired that he was looking to form a band around the name and around that instrumental track, 'The Selecter.' And he had worked with quite a few musicians who were in Hard Top 22 before anyway. I was really the only person he didn't know. And I guess it was just one of those serendipity things. All the people who were in that room that night would go on to have a top ten single in about four months time," Black says.

But before their first single debuted, the Selecter got together, rehearsed hard, and wrote their songs. "It was collaborative in the respect that if somebody had a good idea or they had a song like the top line of something and some words, then you would obviously bring it to the band and go from there. The band would say, 'Yeah, I can add this bass line,' or stuff like that, so it was collaborative in that way. But we didn't all sit around and come up with a song as a collective. Like the initial idea or the initial start would come from an individual and then you'd bring it into the band. That's how I got the band to work on two songs that I had written, 'Black & Blue' and 'They Make Me Mad' which are both on the *Too Much Pressure* album," says Black.

In only three weeks time, with heavy writing and heavy rehearsing, the Selecter hit the road and performed for their first time together as a band, playing at the Electric Ballroom in London on the same bill as the Specials and Madness. Then they hit the road on a 40-gig tour with the other two bands, bringing the 2Tone sound to every nook and cranny of England.

We were touring with the Specials almost immediately. When "On My Radio" came out it went top ten in the pop charts in October 1979. That happened while the Selecter was on the 40 date Tone tour with the Specials and Madness. After a few weeks, Madness left to tour America and for a short period of time Dexy's Midnight Runners joined the tour. We were playing 2,000 capacity venues and they'd be absolutely packed houses. There'd be sweat dripping off the ceiling, people jumping off balconies. The venues were like old dance halls. There was a whole load of those kind of clubs that were still around then and it was just absolutely crazy. Each band did an hour set, so that was three hours of music that people got to listen to, all high energy and it was just a really really crazy time. All of the bands, all three of them, had seven people in them, plus all the roadies and fans, just whoever was around. They were phenomenal times and we all traveled in the same bus and, ah, it was exciting!"

The band had to very quickly learn the music business, something of which they had little knowledge. After all, there was much more to music than just performing.

Back in those days, to a certain extent, I wouldn't say we were naïve, but it was definitely a very very steep learning curve. We asked Juliet de Vie to manage us. At the time, she worked for Trigger, the Specials' PR company, which was owned by the Specials' manager Rick Rogers. It just made sense to have a female manager. She was only 21 at the time. She had no experience in managing a band, so people might think we were crazy allowing such a thing to happen, you know, that you're supposed to go for a much more tried and tested older person who has some experience with dealing with lawyers and accountants. But no, we just jumped in with both feet and said, "Yeah, come aboard, that sounds really good, we're all learning, you learn too." So maybe that was slightly insane, but it made for some interesting times.

Most of the writing for the band's songs was done by Neol Davies. In fact, when Davies formed the Selecter, he had already written most of the band's classic songs, including "Too Much Pressure," "On My Radio," "Missing Words," and "Three Minute Hero." And like the other 2Tone bands paid homage to the Jamaican greats who paved the way for ska, so too did the Selecter honor the Jamaican founders with two covers on their first album, including "Carry Go Bring Come" by Justin Hinds and "Time Hard" by the Pioneers. Black recognizes the link between the two eras of music, yet acknowledges the differences.

I think it was probably a complete mystery to them [Jamaican artists] what we were doing. We were taking the ska beat and the ska sound, but obviously it was a much more contemporary sound, and I remember at that time, I think, Desmond Dekker was doing some stuff, I know he was, and also Toots and the Maytals came over and they did a live show, I can't remember, it was either at Hammersmith Odeon or Hammersmith Palais or somewhere. It was at a London venue, and they recorded the concert and it went straight to vinyl and it was out on the streets being sold within 24 hours and that was a really big deal, and we thought, "Wow," you know, Toots and the Maytals had come over. There was a sudden resurgence in the ska sound and they immediately came over to Britain and obviously wanted to be a part of that, which I thought was brilliant, because all of the young people who were around didn't know the kind of sources we were referencing at the time.

And as their career quickly progressed, as ska became a new version of the old sound, and as the Jamaican ska greats experienced a rebirth, the Selecter found themselves touring with their idols, many of whom were ska stars as well as reggae artists. "It was wonderful to meet them. The old guys like the guys in the Skatalites were actually saying something about life in Jamaica. You can't but dance to it. There's nothing else you can really do, it makes you feel good. At that time, you still had people like Bob Marley touring and so there was a whole kind of reggae scene as well, I mean Aswad, Steel Pulse, Third World, all those bands were around, so it was just like this wonderful off-beat soup everywhere. It was really good," Black says.

And it was good, for a short time. But soon the members of the Selecter became disenchanted with the 2Tone label, seeing the out-of-control merchandising and marketing of the label instead of the creative power promised. The group announced their departure from the 2Tone label in late 1980 with a statement to the press saying that their ideas had been hampered. Black says the label just couldn't accomplish what they had hoped it could.

It just became too unwieldy and I think people had high ideals for the 2Tone label which were talked about, but didn't really happen. For a label to really have any clout, it has to be financially viable. In reality the 2Tone label was a great logo and a great image, but we were still part of a corporate machine, which was Chrysalis Record Company, and if they wanted to put their little butterfly logo all over our records, then they could. We had to jump to their tune rather than they jumped to ours. It is important for an independent label to be allowed to make some mistakes as well as successes. A large record company can afford to make mistakes. But when you're a small label and you sign a new band and it doesn't do particularly well first time around, then you've got a problem, when it's time to get money out of the record company for other signings. Suddenly they won't pay up.

The Selecter then signed directly to Chrysalis and cut a deal just like 2Tone. The Selecter's label didn't have a name, just a logo because they didn't like the Chrysalis butterfly logo.

The logo was adapted by Jane Hughes, who was at the time the wife of Neol Davies. It was adapted from a government utility symbol that was used in Britain during the Second World War. It was decided that the logo was a kind of trademark for an "of the people and for the people" kind of idea. The colors of black, white, and red summed up the racial configuration of the band and the color of our particular brand of politics at the time. We didn't have the chance to sign any other bands to our label because we split up nine months after signing to Chrysalis. We signed to Chrysalis because we felt we were being stifled within the 2Tone label. It was sad, but it was necessary to gain some independence from the Specials and the original idea of all 14 members of us and the Specials being creative directors behind the label had got lost somewhere along the way. We tried to stay true to the idea, but in the end we were cutting off our noses to spite our faces, as they say.

The Selecter hit Horizon Studios in Coventry once again and released their second album, *Celebrate the Bullet*, which came out in February 1981. But this album, in addition to the label change, also saw a lineup change. Keyboardist Desmond Brown left the band for personal reasons and bassist Charley Anderson was asked to leave, both departing before their second album was recorded. "Desmond left the band soon after we returned from our first tour of the States and while we were recording 'The Whisper'/'Train to Skaville' single. He never gave a reason, but unfortunately has suffered ever since with psychiatric problems. Charley Anderson was sacked from the band, by me, because everybody else was too chicken to do it. Charley was trying to push the band towards a reggae direction and Neol Davies was trying to push the band in a rockier direction. As the Jamaican saying goes, 'Two bulls can't rule in one pen.' One of them had to go. Since Neol Davies was the main songwriter and Charley Anderson was not, the outcome was a no-brainer. Charley was much missed from the visual element of the band, as indeed was Desmond," says Black. Brown and Anderson formed their own band,

145

**World War II British utility symbol that was the inspiration for Jane Hughes'
creation of the Selecter logo.**

along with Silverton Hutchinson, former drummer for the Specials. Their
band, the People, released a single, "Music Man," on Race Records, the
label created by John Bradbury, the second former drummer for the Specials. The song was a tribute to Rico Rodriguez. "Together they formed
a new band called the People who did a show for the Anti-Nazi League
in Coventry, quite an infamous show because the National Front were
also marching in Coventry on that day and there was quite a lot of violence on the streets. The People did not last very long unfortunately,"
she says. Brown and Anderson were replaced by James Mackie on keyboards and Adam Williams on bass, but much of the original magic was
gone. The album, *Celebrate the Bullet*, had a less lively sound and didn't
sell as well as their first album, especially in the U.S. Their first single
off the album was the title track, "Celebrate the Bullet," released at a
very inopportune time. Although just a coincidence, the song was
released just after President Ronald Reagan was shot by John Hinckley,
Jr. during an assassination attempt on March 30, 1981. Needless to say,
the song got hardly any airplay in the U.S. The video they filmed for the
song also suffered the same fate, much to Chrysalis' disappointment, as
well as the disappointment of the band. Good timing had once been the
band's success, but now bad timing seemed to work against the band. A
short time later, in 1982, the Selecter called it quits.

> It was all the end of an era [says Black]. I left the Selecter, mainly
> because we'd had a lineup change and I didn't particularly like the two

new people who came into the band, and just the usual musical differences that you go through, and also you have to remember that 2Tone was this brief blip at the end of the punk movement lasting only a couple of years before the New Romantics took over, when bands like Yazoo (known in the U.S. as Yaz) and Duran Duran suddenly became popular. Our music became passé and the whole movement just died for a few years, completely. The music audience in Britain is very fickle. I think that it is less so in America. I think people are more inclined to stick with bands in America if they like them, and therefore there is some longevity for musicians.

And so it did go on, for both the Selecter and Pauline Black. Pauline Black recognized her calling in performing and took little time off, signing a contract right away with Chrysalis for solo work. She recorded a single, "I Can See Clearly Now," a cover of the classic Jimmy Cliff song from the movie, *The Harder They Come*, and a further tribute to the Jamaican founders of the music Black appreciated and loved. "I left the band in 1982 and spent ten years presenting for TV and radio and acting, both on stage and in film. I presented a show called *Black on Black* for three years on TV over here, I won the Time Out/01 for London award for my portrayal of legendary jazz artist Billie Holiday in 1990. Then I re-formed the Selecter in 1991," Black says.

The reformation of the Selecter not only brought back the old sounds of the original band, but put them on the same bills as their Jamaican idols and founders of the music.

Neol Davies and I were approached by three people who had recently left Bad Manners. They asked Neol and myself, would we like to re-form the band. So we tried it out on a tour in America in 1992 and we had a really good time. Then we were invited to go to Japan and play alongside Prince Buster and Lord Tanamo and the Skatalites, and all the originals were there then, Tommy McCook was still alive and Roland Alphonso was still around and it was absolutely fantastic. That was the first time I had been to Japan and Japanese audiences are a bit of a mystery anyway. They're so enthusiastic about the music and so into how they look and how they dress. They absolutely have the whole rude boy, rude girl image down to a tee, or certainly did when we were there and also had their own ska bands, and that was a total revelation and really it was the first time I'd seen the Skatalites play and the first time I'd ever met Prince Buster. It was like, "Wow!" We played Tokyo and Osaka and Nagoya and from that, we got very friendly with Prince Buster. Later we recorded Prince Buster's song "Madness" and I was very honored to sing a duet with him. It was later released as a limited edition single. And we stayed friends with him and he played with us again when we visited Miami because he lives in Miami and got on stage with us in 1997 when we were over touring America. So that relationship has gone on. And then in 1993 we took part in the Skavoovie Tour alongside the Skatalites and the Special Beat, who were an amalgam of some of the members of the Beat and some of the members of the Specials. Some nights we'd headline, some nights Special Beat would headline, and some nights the Skatalites would headline and I think the Skatalites were still pretty much intact on that too. Roland was still there, even though he had had a stroke by that time and he wasn't very well, but he could still play fantastically. Such a beautiful man.

The Selecter was primarily a live band after their initial breakup. They released live albums of their tours in the later years, but they also recorded four studio albums, *The Happy Album* in 1994, *Hairspray* in 1995, *Pucker!* in 1995, and *Cruel Britannia* in 1998.

The other members of the Selecter also had their own careers aside from the band. Neol Davies and the Specials' former bassist Horace Panter formed the band Box of Blues. Davies and Panter pursued their interest in blues music,

Pauline Black, photographed in 2009, continues to perform in a variety of genres, including ska and jazz (photograph courtesy Pauline Black).

releasing albums on the VoMatic Records label, founded and owned by Davies. Davies still flavors some of his tunes with ska and he has recorded the traditional ska song "Come of Age," co-written by Floyd Lloyd, the Alpha Boys School graduate known for his reggae and ska compositions and collaborations with numerous other artists.

Charley Anderson worked with a Swedish ska band called the Skalatones and formed another band with H, or Charlie Bembridge, called the Century Steel Band. Arthur "Gaps" Hendrickson returned for the re-formed version of the Selecter and other 2Tone reunions.

Pauline Black continues to perform as a solo artist. She enjoys "putting the soul into 2Tone." She often likes to take in other genres of music. In recent years she toured with "Homage to Nina Simone & Billie Holiday" with her *Blue Jazz Trio* and with legendary soul singers Geno Washington and Eddie Floyd on the UK "This Is Soul Tour." For Black, the role of the female is very important, which is why she continues to pay tribute to the strong women she admires. They are not unlike her. And strong women in ska were a rarity in such a male-dominated scene. Black women were even rarer. She says:

> I don't think men are particularly keen on a woman who has got forthright opinions. No one has actually put their foot down or stood in my way and said you can't do that, but I think that the main problem is that women are expected to conform to stereotypes and if you buck that tradition, which I did in the Selecter, then sometimes life can be hard going. I wasn't the only one at that time, I mean there were people like Chrissie Hynde, she was very forthright and led her own band, but I think as far as black women are concerned, black women were either supposed to be Tina Turner, so you could be very sexy and raunchy, or you were supposed to go the Diana Ross route and wear lovely dresses and have glamorous flowing long hair. I decided to wear a tonic suit and pork pie hat, it was considered very strange at the time. As a woman I was expected to exploit my sexuality to sell records. That was not for me. But I don't really regret that at all because I think if you're going to do something you might as well put your stamp on it in and carve out a territory that is your own. These days I'm very glad that I did that. My image is unique.

Beyond the impact on women, Pauline Black and the Selecter, as well as the 2Tone concept, had an impact on race relations still today.

"I consider that 2Tone was a brilliant exercise in race relations. The black and white logo is such a vivid emblem of what was behind the music, black people and white people uniting together not only in terms of the colors of their skin, but in terms of the way that they felt about society's ills. The image was inclusive not only of color, but of gender. I think we got that idea across in our music. And I think that people understand that idea has to be revisited again and again — if not the music then certainly that kind of inclusiveness and togetherness, because we live in such a society at the moment which is deliberately, in some ways, trying to split everybody up and make people antagonistic against each other," she says. Certainly the messages in 2Tone's music are eternal and personal. "When new audiences discover those songs, I hope the message can be learned anew by a different, younger generation. They will be our legacy," Black says.

CHAPTER NINE

Welcome to the House of Fun:
Lee "Kix" Thompson of Madness

IT WAS A GOOD THING that Lee Thompson had two friends to set him straight. It was the mid '70s in Camden Town, a neighborhood on the north side of London. For years, Camden was a place of alternative culture, not unlike an East Village in New York City during its heyday, or Haight Ashbury in San Francisco. Members of every subculture group could be found in Camden's markets and clubs — punks, mods, skins, and rockers. Here it was easy to get into trouble. Serious trouble. After 13 times in front of a court for stealing, or as the Brits call it, "nicking," Thompson's final straw with the legal system happened on his birthday, October 5, 1971, when he stole a purse from an employee's locker at a nearby hospital. He was sent away to a reform school for a year (the subject of his song, "Land of Hope and Glory"). He made sure he didn't end up going the way that many of his friends went, into a lifetime of institution after penitentiary, and he made sure he didn't end up going down the same road as his father, who spent 25 years in jail before he died at the age of 57. Thompson became friends with schoolmates Mike Barson and Chris Foreman, friendships that would completely change Thompson's course in life.

Together, Thompson (born in Kentish Town on October 5, 1957), Barson (born in Edinburgh on April 21, 1958), and Foreman (born in London on August 8, 1955), formed a gang named after a club they attended afterschool called the Aldenham Boys Club. "T'was a youth club opened in the early '60s by English Liverpudlian swooner Frankie Vaughan, as his favorite charity was the National Association of Boys' Clubs. This is where local boys and girls would meet up several evenings a week and get involved with a variety of mainly sports and musical activities," says Thompson.

He says he and his friends were different than many of the other kids at the club, who were typically into the soul scene. "There would be the end of the term dance ('73-'74 era) to the likes of Barry White, the Stylistics, or Roxy Music and Bowie. The main fashion of the day was 'soul boy casuals.' Chris Foreman, Mike Barson and myself used to dress different — painted boots and old denim Levi's, and our hair was sometimes colored. We used to have this implement from Woolworth's that held razors that would wreck your barnet or mop [British terms meaning hair]. We would go into our local launderette at Highgate Road and cut each other's hair and take an occasional spin in the tumble drier!" says Thompson.

Lee "Kix" Thompson, saxophone player and co-founder of Madness, originally known as the North London Invaders (photograph courtesy Thompson, from his private photograph album).

And the boys got into their share of mischief at the club as well, which was very much a part of the band's fabric and personality. "On one occasion, some of the Highbury Gang came over from Islington to the club for a confrontation and Barson was in the wrong place at the wrong time on the dance floor. Also, I suppose it was because he's a tall fellow, this little thug went for the biggest target. He had to jump up to make solid contact," says Thomspon. And as these raucous episodes did take place from time to time, the Aldenham Boys Club helped to solidify the boys as comrades, introduced a future relationship, and established a creative union. "I met up with my 'wife to be' there. It was where I felt comfortable with my local pals. I soon got pulled along with Chris to Mike's house to play a bit of rock 'n' roll music," Thompson says.

So the band, which they named the North London Invaders, started as a way for the three friends to just hang out and to stay out of trouble. Thompson was a self-taught saxophone player with no formal musical training or background. "I don't have many early music memories. We never had a radio. I would catch the odd show like *Juke Box Jury*, which was mainly gray, pre-conscription stuff, cheesy. I was out playing whatever chance I could get," Thompson says. Much of his musical tastes were acquired at Chafford School, the reform school where he was sent away. He bought a saxophone which he traded for a clarinet, but then purchased a Selmer Mk6, a tenor saxophone, which he taught himself to play by going out to the cornfield behind his parents' home in Luton, where they had moved.

Mike Barson, known also as Barso, was like many little brothers who idolize their older brothers. He was drawn to music because his brother Danny was a vocalist in a band called Bazooka Joe, along with the future Adam Ant. Barson's other brother, Ben, was also a musician, performing with Clive Langer and the Boxes as well as Kate Bush. So it was a natural step for Mike Barson to follow in his brothers' footsteps. Barson taught himself how to play piano. He did go to art school, but dropped out of Hornsey Art College after one year, taking his art to town, along with Thompson and Foreman, by spray-painting their graffiti on brick walls around Camden.

Chris Foreman, known as Chrissy Boy, was also raised in a musical household. He went to Owens Grammar School in Islington at the same time as the members of Spandau Ballet and was in a class with their manager, Steve Dagger. Foreman's father was a respected folk singer who taught his son rural tunes, although Foreman preferred music with more of an edge. So the three Camden boys worked together as landscapers by day and performed together in their free time and at night, Barson on the keyboards, Thompson on the saxophone, and Foreman on guitar. "Mike's house was perfect for what we were doing. It's where we could thrash out songs, make a cup of tea, and have a laugh or chat without checking the clock every five minutes," says Thompson.

They put together a few songs and they were ready to perform. "Within a year we had a half decent set of covers together and that we were itching to go live with," Thompson says. So they enlisted the help of fellow friend John Hasler to perform on drums and hit the stage. But as was typical in those early days, gigs got a bit rowdy. "At one gig, our drummer was hit by a party 7, which is a very large tin can that holds seven pints of warm alcoholic liquid. It caught him smack on the temple. But slightly dazed and tearful, through rage, he soldiered on and became our singer shortly after," says Thompson.

The band went though changes and additions before reaching their final lineup. During one of their performances at a friend's house, Si Birdsall, two members of the audience, who were also fellow members of the Aldenham Boys Club, began their affiliation with the group. In the audience that day, on June 30, 1977, was Carl Smyth, known as Chas Smash, and Graham McPherson, known as Suggs.

Suggs was born in Hastings on January 13, 1961. An only child, he was uprooted frequently during his childhood since his father left him when he was young and his mother decided to pursue her career as a jazz singer and moved to London. They then moved to Liverpool for a while when Suggs' mother had a residency at a club called The Blue Angel which was run by Alan Williams, the Beatles' first manager. They moved a few more times before Suggs, who failed to get into art school, met up with the boys in the band that summer day at Birdsall's house. He auditioned to be vocalist of the group with an admittedly terrible rendition of "See You Later Alligator."

Thompson describes how he and McPherson took their nicknames, "Kix" and "Suggs" respectively. "There was a newspaper feature on New York subway graffiti, which inspired Chris, Mike, myself, and some pre-band friends to brighten up the grey days by painting smashed up cars and various derelict buildings and brick work. We once covered my old school assembly hall that was left for ages then repaired but still can be seen in certain sunlight. 'Suggs' was from a jazz book of various artists. He got a pin and the name of Suggs was pin pricked. Mine was a variant on the proper spelling. It was originally spelled Kyx681 which was my house number when I lived for a spell outside of London," says Thompson. The graffiti tag, "Kix," can still be seen on some locations in Camden.

Chas Smash was born Cathal Joseph Patrick Smyth on January 14, 1959, in London, but his father was in the oil business and so the family moved around a lot during Smash's youth, from Ireland, to England, and the Middle East. Cathal never really went by his given name, an Irish moniker, and instead went by Carl until the early band days, when he received a postcard from John Hasler, their original drummer, that was addressed to Chas Smash for unknown reasons, and the name stuck. Smyth's father was not only in the oil business, but he and his wife, Chas Smash's mother, were also competitive Irish dancers, although Chas Smash never went near a dance floor until he was 17 years old. But Smyth would also live a life as a dancer, on stage for Madness as the creator of the group's "Nutty Dance," and emcee, mascot, merchandiser, and a vocalist. However, in the early days, Smyth was recruited to be the group's bass player, which didn't last long since he didn't know how to play. He was replaced by Mark William Bedford, known to Madness fans and friends as Bedders.

Bedders was born in Holloway, North London, on August 24, 1961. He was introduced to the group by classmate Gary Dovey in 1977 when Dovey tried his hand at drumming for the group after John Hasler turned to vocals and then managing the group. Dovey also left for good after he and Thompson got into a fight, which was not uncommon for the members of the band. But Bedders was a worthwhile acquisition, a talent beyond his youth, influenced by his love for Motown and the Beatles.

With Dovey gone, refusing to work with Thompson after their fight, the group still needed a drummer. The position was soon filled by Daniel Woodgate, a friend of Bedders who had come to one of the Invaders' gigs. Woodgate, known as Woody, was born on October 19, 1960, in Camden Town where he was raised. Always talented at art, Woodgate's first job was designing advertising for a shopping center called Whiteley's in Queensway, which helped pay for his first drum kit. Woodgate played drums in a heavy metal band with his brother, but when he heard about the vacancy in the Invaders, he auditioned and the other members reluctantly brought him on board since they weren't sure his shy personality and his different musical tastes were a good fit for the band. But Woody and Bedders were not only great friends, they also meshed musically, so Woody became the last member of the group and by New Year's Day 1979, the ever-changing lineup was solid and complete.

The band took almost as many name changes in the early days as they did lineup changes before settling on Madness. "The Invaders was a name Mike had suggested. We changed this to the North London Invaders, as another band were already on the circuit with this name. We tossed a few names about, one being Morris & the Minors, a name after our trusty ex-royal mail post office vans that transported our amps and instruments around London. Chris eventually came up with the name that stuck good and proper to today. It was under our noses all the time and the title of a track that was in our set list of songs. Ironically, Chrissy Boy was the only one that at first said, 'I didn't really mean for you to take my suggestion seriously!'" says Thompson.

The name Madness was much more than a name though. It was both a reflection of the mix of seven personalities in the band, as well as a nod to the foundation upon which their special blend of musical styles was built. "Madness" was also the name of the 1963 hit by Prince Buster. "Buster was a big influence from as far back as 1970 when I first heard 'Big 5' and 'Al Capone,'" says Thompson. "His lyrics were comical, tongue-in-cheek, but had serious undertones," he says.

It was that influence and sound, combined with the comedy and levity that became the signature sound of Madness. And the sound was just beginning to catch on. At one of England's Rock Against Racism concerts at the famed Hope and Anchor club, Thompson, Suggs, and Smyth attended as aficionados of the styles of music that typically fit the bill. One of the performers at that show was the Special A.K.A. whose sound was strangely akin to that of Madness. Suggs immediately recognized the connection and after the gig he spoke to the Special A.K.A. keyboardist and founder Jerry Dammers, hoping to establish a relationship. In June 1979 Madness was asked to join the Special A.K.A. at a gig, which made even more apparent the similarity in sound, a sound that was poised to take over England.

Realizing their own potential, Madness went into the studio to record a few songs in an attempt to secure a record deal. They recorded three tracks — "The Prince," a tribute to Prince Buster that Thompson wrote; "My Girl;" and the song for which they are named, "Madness." They recorded the demo at Pathway Studios in Highbury. Jerry Dammers was so sure of Madness's potential, he inked a deal with them to record "The Prince" as 2Tone's second single, second to the Special A.K.A.'s own "Gangsters," also greatly influenced by Prince Buster. "The Prince" was released on August 10, 1979, solidifying the 2Tone stronghold. But it would be the only song Madness would record on the 2Tone label.

Although their single charted well, and their short 2Tone tour with the Specials and the Selecter was successful, Madness longed for something different. They signed a contract to record an album with Stiff Records, a label that also recorded Ian Dury and Elvis Costello & the Attractions. The label gave Madness the freedom to branch out more creatively, something that was critical to the Madness image and sound. "We were not particularly keen to sign to 2Tone, even if we could have. We went for Stiff Records who seemed a little more eccentric and met our requirements in the artistic freedom department," Thompson says. Artistic freedom is exactly what the group ordered up and delivered, says Thompson. "Ska, reggae, Motown, soul, doo wop, progressive rock, heavy metal, Cuban beats, Hungarian Jewish music — Madness has a wide influence," he says. However, ska was the order of the day, namely because Madness was attracted to its simple beauty. "Ska was, like '50s rock 'n' roll, though off beat. It was relatively easy to play and one of many influences. Also, no one else was playing this in the U.K. around '76–'77," Thompson says.

Stiff supported Madness's eclectic repertoire. They immediately began recording Madness and the classic album *One Step Beyond* was the result. Madness set off immediately to tour England and then the U.S. for a five-city tour as part of Sire Record's U.S. distribution. But, typical of ska tours in the U.S. in the early '80s, the tour did not go well, so they returned home where 2Tone fever was in full swing. And Thompson says there was never a rivalry between bands, only the good fortune of success. "In all the hectic fanaticism that is entertainment, I personally got on with everyone, but then, I'm that kind of guy. If I get a bad feeling about someone through a clash of personality, I walk. With various types of drink and drugs going around at the time, one can get antagonistic. Fortunately everyone was most civil under the circumstances. The only hiccup was when Chris was confronted by a member of the Selecter but this was defused as quick as it was started. Great days," Thompson says.

But Stiff was careful to market Madness differently than other ska bands, seeing that ska might just be a passing fancy of the fickle English music crowd. Sire Records, who distributed *One Step Beyond* in the U.S. sent a press release stating, "To call Madness strictly a ska band is a mistake," especially in a country that was far from embracing the genre. In fact, the release contained a footnoted definition of ska to inform the reader, stating it was "a pre-reggae form of Jamaican music, also known as bluebeat, skank and rocksteady." The release continued, "While most of their music has a definite rock steady beat, there's also a strong R&B and even straight rock edge to several of their songs." The American public likely wasn't familiar with the term rock steady, but they knew rock, and wasn't that the same? Sire was banking on it. The release concluded, "Music lovers coast-to-coast can discover the 'old' but incredible sound of bluebeat/R&B/rock performed by Madness."

Perhaps those early marketing efforts helped to keep Madness alive while the 2Tone movement died. And, to be fair, Madness did branch out from the ska sound. But even when their albums contained a variety of non-ska sounds, like the hugely popular "Our House" or the cover song "It Must Be Love," Madness still stayed close to what they loved and the ska sound sustained. *Complete Madness*, a compilation of greatest hits released in April 1982 contained a new single, which became the band's first number one hit and continued Madness's ska roots. "House of Fun" propelled Madness forward during a time when other ska bands were treading water and drowning in England.

What most listeners visualize when they think of Madness is perhaps the one characteristic that contributes to the band's survival above all others — a characteristic that many also use to condemn the band and dismiss them despite their successes and longevity — their novelty. Early in the band's creation, Lee Thompson invented the band's "Nutty Sound," which he describes.

> I wanted a type of music that was not commercially interested but quirky. A little bit Frank Zappa (who came along to see us in New York in 1980) but not as intellectual as Frank, simply because we were not the

best of musicians. I also pulled from *Steptoe & Son*, a very British sitcom, so as not to pigeonhole us into a certain genre. It had a very music hall/British sound. I tried to put all this across in a song that is on the flipside of the 12" *One Step Beyond* release. Mike was a prominent writer in the band and had a knack, or rather a gift, for writing hits that Stiff simply adored, so that "Nutty Sound" was something I could really experiment with on the flipsides. The lyrics to this sound would be, again, quirky such as "Don't you eat That yellow snow" [Frank Zappa] or "Little Egypt" [the Coasters], or the Sensational Alex Harvey Band's track "N.E.X.T." about a mobile army whorehouse, or Alice Cooper's "Love It to Death" or "Billion Dollar Babies." Priceless.

That sense of humor, that "Nutty Sound" and image, became the foundation of the band. That sense of humor was also a very British creation, akin to Monty Python or Benny Hill to U.S. audiences, requiring an explanation from Sire Records in the U.S. in their press release. Sire described the group's act as "a touch of cabaret" and cites Thompson explaining his Nutty creation as "a sort of happy fairground sound with jokey lyrics."

Certainly those lyrics were "jokey." No subject was off limits for the band that chose fun over the politics of other bands. The song "Baggy Trousers" detailed the fun times in school. The hit tune "Our House" described the crazy comings and goings of a large family, and "House of Fun" was about a boy who just turned 16 and patronizes a "chemist," an English term for a drug store, in an attempt to buy condoms. Or the silly "Chipmunks Are Go!" which is simply a cheer. Others tell stories of an oar man floating down the River Nile, Tarzan's nuts, a loafer who slept on a sofa, a man who has lived with his mother for forty years, Michael Caine, three cheers for a blue skinned beast, and most recently a tune about early turn-of-the-century London. Madness's music was a far cry from the politics and racial advice of other ska groups. Perhaps in the economic hardship of the Thatcher era, fans were just looking to have a little fun, with music's sound as well as content, and the Nutty Boys were happy to oblige. They brought their fun antics to television audiences numerous times, on the usual *Top of the Pops* and on the British show *TISWAS*, a live children's show broadcast from 1974 to 1982. *TISWAS* was an acronym for This Is Saturday Watch And Smile. They also performed at the Prince's Trust Gala, playing the British national anthem on kazoos, and they performed on the classic British show *The Young Ones*, which was broadcast on MTV in the U.S., further establishing Madness's international popularity.

But the band's longevity was more than just a fun, crossover sound that appealed to audiences young and old. Madness also was able to survive by weathering some very difficult storms. Perhaps the biggest blow to the band was the departure of founding member and key songwriter Mike Barson. Just before the band was about to leave for a huge U.S. tour in 1983, Mike Barson missed an appearance on a scheduled television show in Germany, which was uncharacteristic for him. He did, however, perform all 25 gigs in the U.S., playing with the likes of David Bowie and the Police. But the success may have just been too much for Barson who announced his departure when the boys returned home. The impact was great. "Being a prominent writer, this hit the band, but more so, our mate was jumping ship. We were going through big changes. Our record company was about to merge with Chris Blackwell at Island. Mike was into his Buddhist practice and the band was taking up too much of his time. He was living in Amsterdam which was only across the pond, but this made things difficult. I think at the time it was a good time for a sabbatical and his choice. As for the rest, we trudged on, signed to Virgin and released a pretty good album *Mad Not Mad*," Thompson says. Barson played his last performance as part of a Greenpeace benefit show on December 21, 1983, before permanently moving to Amsterdam.

But Madness was able to sustain despite the departure of Barson, signing to a much larger label, Virgin Records, which allowed the band to have the same arrangement as many other ska bands had with their labels. The members of Madness wanted to create their own label under the Stiff umbrella, but Stiff boss Dave Robinson said no, so they sought a company that would say yes. Virgin allowed Madness to have their own label, which the band called Zarjazz, and they put out their first single, "Listen to Your Father" by Feargal Sharkey, which was written by Chas Smash. But the *Mad Not Mad* album was the prize of the relationship with Virgin and the band members put a lot of effort into making it a quality production, backed by ample Virgin funding. The band recruited Jerry Dammers to fill Barson's vacancy on the album, and although

Thompson and many other listeners felt the album was a fantastic product, others, including Suggs, were critical. "Suggs described it as a 'polished turd,'" says Thompson. Still, the band took up touring, enlisted French horn player and Rico Rodriguez's friend Dick Cuthell. But the album production was expensive, and touring expensive too. With album sales low and with no hits produced, the band found themselves owing Virgin money rather than making it. And to top it off, the band members had very different views on where the group should go next.

So in September 1986, the boys decided to call it quits. But the "Nutty Sound" refused to die. There were many other incarnations and reformations over the years, including a band called the Madness, as well as the Nutty Boys. There were numerous compilations and reissues and tours. There were secret reunions and official reunions and even new albums. Thompson says today he can't even recall the reason they originally split. "We have had so many comebacks, more than Frank Sinatra supposedly, that I have clean forgot," says Thompson when asked why they broke up so many times.

Those changes brought Madness closer to ska's Jamaican roots, coming full circle. In 2005, Madness released an album called *The Dangermen Sessions*. Gigs surrounding the release of this album included tunes by Lord Tanamo, Roland Alphonso, Desmond Dekker, Tommy McCook, Ken Boothe, Max Romeo, and of course, Prince Buster. The single release from the album, "Shame and Scandal," is a Jamaican classic.

What keeps Madness returning to the stage more than anything else, however, is the loyal Madness fan. Even nuttier than the Nutty Boys themselves are the nutty fans. On January 1, 1981, the Madness Fan Club released their first issue of the *Nutty Boys Madness Comix*. The publication printed by the Madness Information Service, as the club called themselves, featured comic strips of the band members and the story of their creation under the headline, "Madness is Born." Photos; sketches by fans; and information on each band member, such as their favorite food and "If you could be someone else, who would it be?" elicited responses like the "Ei Atolla" [*sic*] from Suggs and "Superman" from Chrissy Boy. The Madness Information Service still exists today with blow-by-blow commentary on everything Madness and archived material from the past 30 years, including a thorough archive of Madness articles and publications.

Perhaps the most astounding feat revealing the depth of Madness fan dedication is something that can only be measured and quantified. During their performance at Madstock, a concert held August 8 and 9, 1992, at Finsbury Park, London (as well as in 1994, 1996, and 1998), jumping fans throughout the opening song, "One Step Beyond," literally caused reverberations akin to an earthquake registering 4.5 on the Richter scale. Madness fans are truly "One Step Beyond," encouraging the band to keep performing and recording year after year.

CHAPTER TEN

Fat Bastard: Buster Bloodvessel of Bad Manners

H E STANDS ON STAGE in front of thousands of fans who egg him on. Over 400 pounds, he sticks his enormous tongue out of his mouth like a slice of Christmas ham and waggles it at the audience before grabbing his plate of cheese and pickle sandwiches, a dish only a Brit could love, and devours bite after bite while singing a tune named after the culinary delight. From the flapping mouth of the gigantic, bald, fat man spews chunks of the epicurean display. The crowd goes crazy for the antics of the band's lead singer, knowing full well he is only living up to his band's name. He is Buster Bloodvessel, vocalist for the English band Bad Manners.

Buster Bloodvessel was born Douglas Trendle on September 6, 1958, in Hackney, London. He grew up in a working class family in a typical London household during the '60s and '70s. "My father was always a great reader, and my parents just worked so hard that they didn't really have time for the arts as such. But it's something that was always inside of me that's always said, 'You will do something artistic, there's no doubt about that.' You know, even going through school and things, I always stuck out as a person who was a bit different from everybody else, I suppose," says Trendle.

Trendle certainly was different and he had a penchant for being a bit of a showman. He thought he would pursue a career in acting, but when it came time to spend the 12½ pence in his pocket on an acting class, he chose instead to spend it at a restaurant located across the street from the theater school. But Trendle also had a love for music, growing up with siblings who were part of the cultural and musical scene of the era in London. "My brother was a teddy boy and my sister was a mod," says Trendle.

A teddy boy was sort of a British version of a greaser. They began in the 1950s and wore hairstyles called a "duck's ass" which is slicked back on both sides, meeting at the back. They frequently wore sideburns and looked like a young Elvis Pressley or Jerry Lee Lewis, but with a British flair. Their brightly colored socks were visible under the pant legs of high-waisted trousers. They wore sport coats, sometimes with a velvet collar in latter years, over white dress shirts and a fancy tie, such as a long-tailed bow or a Western-style bolo tie. The style became popular again with the rockabilly resurgence in the 1970s in England.

Mods, on the other hand, were more aligned with the working class but with attention to being hip and dandy. They wore short, cropped hairstyles and girls frequently had their hair short on top with bangs but with long fringes around the face and around the back. Mod boys wore sophisticated suits, crewneck or V-neck sweaters, or button-down collared shirts and thin neckties, while mod girls wore button-down white collared shirts and mini skirts. The mods drove scooters as their choice mode of transportation and wore military parkas to protect their stylish clothes from the elements while riding.

But the teddy boys and mods commonly clashed, culturally as well as physically, brawling at soccer games during the 1960s. And to have a representative of each group in the Trendle household was both bad as well as good for little Doug, whose musical tastes were just developing. Of the groups, Trendle says, "I loved both of their music, so I couldn't make up my mind what I wanted to be so I definitely wasn't going to be any of those. When I grew up I wanted to have my hair very short. In fact, none at all!"

So Trendle and his schoolmates from Woodberry Down Comprehensive School decided to form their own band and things took off quickly.

We all went to school together and it sort of started with a trip to Stonehenge, on which we all got very drunk, and most of them were musicians and were going to play at the free festival that they used to have and well, I just decided that I'd become the singer cause they didn't actually have a singer. So we didn't have a name and we thought of the name Stand Back as we were driving up there. And we got on stage and our first song was called "The Cheese and Pickle Blues," about a big packet of cheese and pickle sandwiches that my mom made me to come on the gig and so I just sung that whole story, my mum making me all these cheese and pickle sandwiches whilst eating all the cheese and pickle sandwiches and singing the blues. And it seemed to work. Basically people were running all around waking people up saying, "You've got to come and see this, it's really funny." And then we went into a couple of ska songs that we'd written, reggae ska songs, and then we did "The Monster Mash" and we left the stage to a huge applause, and we thought, "Well that wasn't bad for our first gig."

He says their music was inspired by a blend of sources both typical and novel.

The early influence was big band sort of bands, like Louis Jordan and Louie Prima and Chuck Berry and Otis Redding and so, very much black music, with a certain amount of humor to it. I mean people like Fats Domino I just adored and just thought they were the best thing ever and of course all of these people that I've just mentioned have been an influence to me. It's quite amazing; you do feed off of your early music that gets to your heart. Kids' music really got to us and film soundtracks, definitely. In fact we loved bands like the Bonzo Dog Doo Dah Band, which to me are just like such an influence to anybody that likes anything with music because it's humorous and it's very hard to be humorous in music. To make music popular and to be humorous is almost unheard of and yet we're one of the people that have achieved that.

Achieve success they did. Trendle took the stage name Buster Bloodvessel, the name of the conductor in the Beatles movie *Magical Mystery Tour*. It was an appropriate name, considering in each performance, Trendle gave it his all and looked as if he might, at any moment, bust a bloodvessel. Harmonica player Alan Sayagg took the crazy name Winston Bazoomies, for unknown reasons; guitarist Louis Cook gave respect to Skatalites legend Roland Alphonso by assuming the name Louis Alphonso; drummer Brian Truitt went by the name Chewit, a play on his last name; bass player David Farren first was called Reggy Mental but then changed names to David Farr-in; tenor saxophonist Chris Kane was simply called Crust; alto saxophonist Andrew Marson was called Marcus Absent; and keyboardist Martin Stewart went by the name Mr. Bogingong. They were a fully marketable group. Gigging around England, they set out to attract a record label, which is exactly what they did. When record executives who attended Bad Manners' gigs walked in, they witnessed staff at the door branding guests with yellow and black striped construction tape, telling them they were now a Bad Manners fan. Impressed with the grass roots marketing effort, and the Bad Manners' sound and appeal, Magnet Records offered them a contract and they signed.

Magnet Records was a very small label, started in 1973 by R.A. Coke in North London. Bad Manners was the biggest band signed to the label, then and ever, before it was sold in 1988 to Warner Bros. Signing to a small label had its benefits and challenges. Although Bad Manners did receive focused attention, the label simply didn't have the money for promotion like bigger labels did. So when Bad Manners released their first album, *Ska 'N' B* in 1980, it was the appeal of the music alone that propelled Bad Manners to success. Merit and wild performances, that is.

"We were always very very popular on *Top of the Pops*. Every single we had that was sort of successful was probably due to our performances that we achieved on *Top of the Pops*. Our record company was too mean to afford to buy, to let us have videos, so they would insist that we just did *Top of the Pops* and any other shows that were going. We would play them live. It was a real shame because everybody was getting real expensive videos. So we decided we've got to do our best on *Top of the Pops* and we can't allow any other band to follow us or to play before us, we've got to stick out as being the most notorious band on there that week, and so we did. We dressed outrageously on every performance we ever did for them," Trendle says.

Among those performances were the outlandish interpretation of their hit song "Lorraine," sung by Buster Bloodvessel dressed up as Henry

166

XIII in a fur cloak with a feather hat and full beard, singing to a blow up doll while Winston Bazoomies jumped around on stage between harmonica solos in a cowboy hat and yellow sunglasses. In 1981 the band's appearance on the show performing their hit "Can Can" had them all dressing as, what else, can can girls, and with Buster Bloodvessel in a skirt with bald head and Doc Marten boots, it's quite a sight. On the German televised performance of the song, Buster Bloodvessel rode through the aisles of the seated crowd on a bicycle dressed like a Frenchman in a striped shirt, black beret, and a loaf of French bread in his bike basket before taking to the stage with the rest of the similarly-dressed band and a line of can can girls. They also performed regularly on the British kids' show *TISWAS*.

Perhaps Bad Manners' most notorious televised performance came not in England, but on live television in Italy, which resulted in a series of events leading to their being banded from the country.

Italian people are quite amazing for us [says Trendle]. We played a festival which was televised, which was not like a festival as we thought of it. We just thought it was going to be a really great festival with a lot of people dancing around and all that. But when we got there it was all full of middle-class, middle-aged people that really didn't understand Bad Manners. They were all sitting there all looking very nice, the way they were dressed, everyone made an effort, and all the presenters all smiled, and we're playing with Barry White and Dire Straits. And so we were on first and so I said, well Barry White's getting it. He's on after us, he's definitely getting it. We can't allow him to be better than us. So we started performing and I could see that these middle-aged, middle-class, middle-of-the-road people would like Barry White more than they would like us. I could see it. So I had to do double the performance. Sometimes when you push a performance it doesn't really work. And so they weren't that impressed. I could see I wasn't really winning, but I really don't like losing. So I decided I would expose my bottom. And I knew I would shock the audience and I would either make them laugh or it would make them cry. And I went close to a camera and I shoved my ass right up there, as close to the camera as I could possibly get it. Of course I ended up offending the whole of Italy. I didn't realize it was such an offensive thing there, but it was even weirder. All of a sudden there was a lot of nervous laughter. It started in the hall. It was a nervous laughter and it spread like wildfire through the whole place. And it made them all nervous and they all started clapping and singing and dancing along with the track then, so it worked. And then Barry White went on and was average after that. And as I walked off the stage, they said to me, "You don't realize what you've done, do you?" I said, "I've only showed me ass, it's alright, we've all got one." It's very true, we all have, but the Pope was watching. They had a real problem with it.

As much as I burst out into laughter about the whole thing and found it rather amusing, it captured an imagination inside the Italian newspaper world. They went crazy on me. Everywhere I went in Italy I was followed by camera crews and photographers all wanting my comments on what I thought about religious things. I'm only doing this for a laugh, mate. It was just quite an amazing situation that I got myself into. They actually climbed the balcony to catch me in bed with somebody. I heard these people outside my balcony and I opened the door and it knocked the ladder and it was falling back, and I looked over the balcony and saw this pile of photographers. It was quite amazing of course, someone said if you want to be really offensive, come and do a photo shoot in a graveyard. I thought, well if that's bloody offensive, I've never heard anything so silly. So I went and had a photograph taken of me in a graveyard. Well then after that we were hounded by the police and they questioned me, like, "Why was I in there defacing the graveyard." "I wasn't defacing it." "You were taking photographs in the graveyard." It's totally illegal. Well it was at the time. And then they put us on this Italian tour that didn't go that well. It was in a sort of disco crowd and they weren't really into ska music. They were into dancing. I suppose, but they weren't really into ska music. It went down a bit strange. And we were put into a chain of hotels which all had English antiques in them. We just started stealing them all. And we were then banned from ever going back to Italy after that. And we've been back since and it's quite amusing because the border patrol people remember that I showed my ass to the Pope.

But for Bad Manners, it was all just entertainment. They were just living up to their name and giving audiences what they came to see, especially during times when people needed an escape. "It was a tough time for Britain, with Margaret Thatcher, the unemployment being at an all time high and nobody having any money. But we made people smile, which is not a bad thing to do. We never wanted to be politicians. We always wanted our music to have fun, and of course that shows you a lot about the songs we've done over the years," Trendle says.

Those songs, hits like "Lorraine" and "Can Can," as well as a cover of Millie Small's tune, this time called "My Girl Lollipop," "Lip Up Fatty," "Walking in the Sunshine," "Special Brew," "Just a Feeling," "Ne-Ne-Na-Na-Na-Na-Nu-Nu," and "Samson & Delilah," took Bad Manners all over the world, touring for fans who came from all over to witness the band's crazy, manic performances.

But a series of events in the mid–'80s and '90s, even into the new millennium, really tested the strength of the band. Winston Bazoomies, Alan Sayagg, began experiencing mental difficulties periodically during times with the band. He took short breaks, but after a nervous breakdown, he was diagnosed as schizophrenic and chose to leave the band. For Trendle, the loss was much more than losing the distinctive sound of the harmonica in Bad Manners' music. It was the absence of a great friend.

> Me and Alan started this whole craziness. He, I suppose, was an inspiration to me and I was very much an inspiration to him in as much as we would get together and he'd send me mad, and then we'd start playing music. He'd send me mad just by laughing and giggling and just getting ourselves in to a really good sense of humor and mood before we'd start listening to this music and then we'd come up with silly little radio programs that we'd make up, on a cassette player, they're sort of like prehistoric now, and they had a microphone with them and that's what we used to do, these radio programs, and make up stories and, just doing nonsense like that, just completely ad libbed, and add music every now and again, which really worked well. And we used to do it that much that when we started touring we would find these cassettes we'd made. I wish we'd kept more. There were so many really brilliant ones, but of course they go by the by. Anyway, him and me went to school together. He taught me to do my laces up and I taught him how to talk. That's how close we were. He couldn't talk properly when we first met. He had a bit of a problem with speech and I taught him to talk properly. It wasn't that hard. But I couldn't do my laces up, my shoelaces. Some boys develop after others and I couldn't do mine up and used to tuck them in. He used to go, "Why do you tuck your laces in?" "I can't do 'em up," so he taught me to do that and I taught him how to speak. That's how close we were. Unfortunately, he had a nervous breakdown, through running the band, I think, more than anything. He was the accountant and he did lots of other bits and pieces. This is when we shared the jobs,

before I took them all on myself. And it was just too much for him. He was always a very humorous man. He's one of the funniest men I've ever met. I mean you would just be in his company and he would make you laugh. It's a great skill. When you've got that so naturally. He was, it was said, a bit like a Tommy Cooper character [a British comedian]. Not the same way of humor when you think about that, but just a natural with his humor. He just can't help himself, he's so naturally funny. Without Alan, I probably wouldn't have pushed because Alan was an influence as well as he was my best friend. At the same time, we influenced each other. Without a doubt, without him, there would have been no Bad Manners. I was the other driving force and the two of us were very strong. And when it came to stage, I was always more dominant than him, yet his secondary role was very strong for us at the time, that's for certain. Unfortunately he had a few nervous breakdowns. He lives at the other side of London, but I know he does really well and I do still see him whenever I can, but because of our jobs and the distance of where we live, I don't see him as much, but he's a happy man. He just doesn't want anything to do with music anymore. And I respect him for that, of course.

But without Sayagg on the Bad Manners payroll, the flavor wasn't the same. And when Bad Manners left Magnet and signed with the much larger Portrait Records, a U.S. label that was an imprint of Epic Records, they may have had money to put behind the next album, but there were enough changes that sales were lower than expected. The album, *Mental Notes* [the word "mental" to the British is synonymous with wild or crazy] was incredibly expensive to produce, yet Portrait Records never distributed the album in the U.K. or Europe, upsetting the bulk of Bad Manners' fans.

It was a tough time when we had split from Magnet and we wanted to go and do our own thing but we wanted it to be different from what we were doing before, but in a similar vein. It's hard to explain that really. We always wanted it to still have the same qualities but different from what we sounded like before. We certainly wanted it to be more professional, but that isn't the right terminology for it, professional. We wanted it to be more produced and more from the producers' point of view rather than the individuals in the band. And I think we used about three producers in all for the making of it. And one of them was Richard Hartley, a character who was very good, a very good chap. He did quite a lot of Western theatre stuff. Nobody thought he was going to be very good at what he did for us, but I always found his work was very good. He was completely different from what we previously had as a producer. I think it's always good to open up and to do what's maybe different and that's what I think we were maybe looking for with that album.

The result was much less of a ska sound and more of a funk and soul sound, a clear diversion for Bad Manners. None of the tunes off of *Mental Notes* did well at all, especially since the album wasn't available in the countries with the most Bad Manners fans and in Bad Manners' homeland. The group found themselves in debt to Portrait due to their production fees and they had to do live performances just to pay them off.

But Bad Manners refused to die, although their leader actually did do just that, for eleven seconds. Trendle tells the tale:

> I started off being quite a large eater slash drinker and of course that swells the body to unimaginable sizes, and I got to the size of 32 stone. I don't know what that is in pounds [it is 448 pounds]. I know it's huge. And I lost 18 to 20 stone [252 pounds to 280 pounds]. That's also very huge. It was down to the fact that I had an operation, but also at the same time as that operation, I also caught meningitis and died for eleven seconds. I was in and out of a coma thereafter for three months. This was only a couple of years ago. At the same time we still gigged. We still kept our dates and didn't want to let anyone down. A few of them I was completely off my trolley, I didn't know where I was, what I was doing. Very very unhealthy part of my life.

Trendle collapsed onstage over ten times while performing during this period. But years of abuse had finally caught up to him. Eating antics onstage were only a show. Real life antics found Trendle consuming 29 Big Macs in a single day on a dare before throwing up all over the restaurant's table; guzzling a huge jar of pickled onions and pork pie shaken into a chunky beverage; and owning Fatty Towers, a hotel that was an alternative to the health and fitness spas of the day and literally catered to those with huge appetites by offering such selections as a four and a half pound meat pudding and tequila slushies.

"I also had a hernia which is why I had to have a gastric bypass, and rather than put a band on me [the doctor] said, 'Well if we do it this way, this way it works and it works forever.' He said, 'You can't cheat it this way and I think you should do it this way.' I went, 'Look, you're the boss. You just tell me what to do. I'll just lie here and do it.' And where he's from he's considered as god, so he basically made a new man out of me. I'm actually very fit and healthy at the moment and very happy with the way things have gone. I'm going to get a tummy tuck next year. I've that to look forward to yet. But from a man who's abused his body his whole life, to now one that looks after it a little bit more, and I think I still give it lots of abuse, I think I'm doing very well," he says.

And a much thinner Buster Bloodvessel continues to tour with Bad Manners all year long, living up to the band's moniker of being the "Hardest Working Band on the Planet." And work hard, Trendle does.

I've always been in charge [he says]. It's a burden and a half because you've got to actually look after and become like Mother Goose to possibly nine or ten, more than that, like 20 people around us at least, I've got to go look after and make sure that they're all doing the right things at the right time, so I've become agent, the tour manager, the manager, the record company, the producer, the cook, the hotelier, just about every job in the world, I have something to do with it, even if it's just shouting at people. We started to run ourselves as a democracy a long time ago but the democracy didn't work. It made things good for individuals, but not so good for others, so people were thinking from their own point of view and not from the band's point of view. And so I had to take it over as a complete dictatorship and run it the way I saw best for the band and not just for the individual, which is how we do run it. It's a hard job because I don't know anybody else that's ever lasted running a band the size we have. I know of bands that are three or four people, but to have a band with a brass section that you use every time. There are about 30 or 40 musicians surrounding Bad Manners, and at any time we can pull on any of them, and we have to do it like that because sometimes we need somebody and sometimes they want to go off and earn more money by playing with somebody else, and so we make it quite acceptable that as long as you're good enough and you can step back in and still be good enough, then you've got the job, you're in the squad, shall I say. It's a bit strange way to run a band but I found it easiest to have more musicians rather than less musicians.

So why continue to endure? Well it's obvious from his performances that Trendle loves what he does, but he also loves the fans and they love him back.

Unbelievable fans with Bad Manners. To be honest, I wouldn't still be doing this if it wasn't for the fans, if it was just my ego, but it's not. It's the fact that Bad Manners fans just love to have a party, so we've held that so long now, being the best party band around, and certainly in the ska world, you know that there's a lot of ska people in the world, and a lot of Bad Manners fans in the crowd, you're guaranteed that that's going to be the best night you'll see in that club, anywhere in the world. It happens all over the world and it's quite amazing, and people don't really understand how much we get that crowd going. With the likes of huge bands around that would come in and play smaller clubs and do an equally same sort of job, but when it comes to ska music, it's just got that extra push that makes you just can't help yourself dancing. Wherever we play they always

Buster Bloodvessel, vocalist and gastronomist for Bad Manners. Buster Bloodvessel is known for his antics, such as dressing up as Henry VIII on *Top of the Pops* and mooning the Pope on Italian television, as much as he is for his classic songs like "My Girl Lollipop," "Lorraine," and "Lip Up Fatty." Buster Bloodvessel underwent gastric bypass surgery in 2004 and is shown here post surgery (photograph courtesy Joe Kerrigan).

say, "Well I've never seen anything like that." And still to this day, I hear wherever we play they've never seen this before. They go, "Well I've never seen anything like that." The crowd just goes so mad. For me, the Bad Manners fan is probably not as lucky as other fans because they don't get too much material released all the time, but the Bad Manners fan I think has benefitted more than any other fan over the years. I don't know many bands who put on as many gigs as us, so we do hold lots of little records. When it comes to things like, if it was down to the amount of sweat produced by one band, I guarantee, we won that, hands down.

CHAPTER ELEVEN

Melting Pot

IT IS SWEET IRONY that the country that put the nail in the coffin for each 2Tone band that crossed the big pond, then became the country that next took the ska torch and carried it on into other genres. Founded upon a tradition of taking all things British and making them uniquely and independently American, it is no wonder then that the ska sound in the U.S. became a part of virtually every other genre of music, a product of a musical melting pot. Ska talent in America was strong and those who found a way to capitalize on the industry, whether through their business savvy, or through their mainstream marketability, brought the ska tradition to bigger and younger audiences.

In the early '80s, English ska was a tough sell in the U.S. Looking back, almost three decades later, Jayson Nugent, guitarist for New York-basked ska band the Slackers offers his explanation of why.

> It had too much of an English sound. A big part of it that a lot of people don't recognize, and instead say, "Oh, America didn't like punk" or "Oh, America didn't like ska," is that America's a much bigger country. We had those things but we had it in cities. We had it in New York, in L.A., San Francisco had those scenes but it just didn't spread to the middle of the country. The music was still a little localized at that point. Britain is a lot smaller of a country. Reggae and stuff like that, a lot of the black population in England is Caribbean, whereas in America, they're not, so there, I think, it's easier for it to catch on because you had Caribbean and Jamaican communities in a lot of cities there. Not that 2Tone was catching on with the Jamaican community, but at least

white kids had a sort of frame of reference. It didn't seem like foreign music to them, whereas to America it seemed kind of foreign. And it's just easier for the music to travel and the bands to travel around. In England you can drive from one side of England to the other in eight hours. It's like New York State, you know? Their vans can tour, you hit a city every hour, the music can spread really quickly. You can get a radio station from London and if you're anywhere in the Midlands or south you can still get a strong signal, and with BBC, you've got a national radio station playing this stuff, so you can reach the whole country. Here you've got local radio stations with local scenes. If something kind of hit they would play it coast to coast but it didn't catch on so quick in the middle of the country. Every region had their thing that was big — country music here, you had disco and soul there, you had more groovy rock getting played here and there. You didn't have a national radio station like the BBC. That's something that people overlook. Even reggae didn't get that big here because people saw it as foreign, but there you had Jamaicans throughout the country, and that's what black England was all about. It was very Jamaican. Whereas in black America it was very Christian southern, so it's a different flavor — soul, gospel, R&B, those kinds of things is what was getting played. The Jamaican influence or really English, was seen as foreign.

But take one of those Brits and implant him and his foreign music here in the U.S. and that, along with the simmering sounds of 2Tone among college students and youth in America, firmly planted the seeds of ska where it branched out, in different regions, with different flavors. That one Brit was Robert Hingley, known to his friends, colleagues, and fans as Bucket.

Bucket came to the U.S. in the early '80s from England, relocating for a work position that wasn't in the music industry, although that very quickly changed when he founded his own band, the Toasters, and his own record label, Moon Ska Records. "The Toasters started back in 1981. I was sent over here to work and I saw English Beat in Roseland back in 1981 and there were about 150 people there and I thought that was absolutely insane. It was at that point that I decided to start a ska band in the U.S.," says Bucket. The band's sound, however, wasn't just a cookie cutter version of the 2Tone bands, whose sounds had already proven a tough sell in the U.S. Instead, Bucket made the sound his own and the other musicians were American and had a very different frame of reference. "The Toasters got their start, not really being influenced by any other ska band, because they weren't exposed to any over here. The guys in the band didn't have a grounding in the 2Tone tradition as I had earlier. For me, there was a lot of stuff, I mean, I was influenced by ska from '64 to '69, Trojan reggae, but also Motown and Delta blues and stuff like that," he says.

The challenge, however, was how to find, not only an audience for this special brew, but more importantly in a capitalistic America, how to find a market and a way to be marketed, to buyers, to radio stations, and to the industry in general. Bucket found the door slammed in his face at virtually every turn, which only made him fight harder for the music he loved. He started his own label in the great do-it-your-self tradition of so many punks before him, and so many after him.

Robert Hingley, better known as Bucket, founded the Toasters and his own ska label, Moon Ska Records, in 1981. He continues to perform with the Toasters and manage his newest music label, Megalith (photograph Heather Augustyn).

I started Moon because nobody else would put out the damn record, essentially. We had this Toasters' EP that was produced by Joe Jackson, it sounded great and nobody was interested in it. I couldn't believe it. Nobody wanted to take a chance on distributing this record, so we put it out ourselves. We got laughed at by pretty much every record company in the country because they didn't think we could do anything with it. I guess they thought that ska music was something that happened in England. It was like this cute sort of funny circus kind of music, and it had been done and they didn't give it any kind of credibility. The other thing that is dangerous about that is how do you market it when it's black people and white people? Do we market it to the white people, or do we market it to the black people? It's confusing for them [says Bucket].

The Moon Ska label soon began distributing many American ska bands in addition to bringing ska imports from overseas for U.S. consumption. They put together numerous ska compilations, the first of which contained a song by the then unknown band, No Doubt. Other bands and musicians that were distributed by Moon Ska Records during their immensely powerful reign until the year 2000 were Laurel Aitken, Lloyd Brevett, Bad Manners, Hepcat, Let's Go Bowling, Tommy McCook & Friends, Mephiskapheles, New York Ska Jazz Ensemble, the Pietasters, the Scofflaws, Isaac Green & the Skalars, Skavoovie & the Epitones, Skinnerbox, and the Slackers, among numerous others. Whereas ska bands in 1980s England honored the Jamaican tradition by naming their bands after the culture, such as the Selecter, a name for a sound system DJ, or the Specials, the name of a one-off hit played by a sound system DJ, ska bands in America too honored the Jamaican tradition set by the Skatalites by naming their bands with a similar ska word play. Band names were as witty and creative as Skapone, Mephiskapheles, the Skalars, Skarface, Ska Capella, Ska Humbug, and Skampton, hailing from Kalamazoo, Michigan. Not only craftiness, but a high-school band nerd toughness were also part of the new equation.

But by the year 2000, Moon Ska Records had suffered a number of setbacks that made it almost impossible to continue, and so they closed their doors, ending a legacy of promotion for almost any band that considered themselves even slightly ska. "It was a combination of reasons," says Bucket today. "Mainly, it was because of the market downturn. We had a lot of returns and a lot of distributors went out of business. And we had a guy that embezzled some money," he says. That guy was manager of the Moon storefront, Noah Wildman, who worked at Moon from 1995 until he was fired in 1999 for allegedly stealing nearly $100,000 in cash and an unknown additional amount in product, according to Bucket. Today, Bucket is still obviously outspoken, yet cloaked, about the episode that resulted in the end of Moon and a bitter lawsuit. On stage, still touring with the Toasters, Bucket lectures his audience on the importance of friends, keeping them close, but keeping enemies in check as well. Perhaps he has Wildman in mind when he emotes to the audience about betrayal, keeping Wildman close by keeping him in his words of warning to others.

The loss of that revenue was devastating to Moon. "So I decided that with all of those things, it was best to really quit while we were ahead and close up while we were sort of in control of the boat. So that was a pretty tough decision, but as it turned out, it was the right one to make. That was 2000," Bucket says. But he quickly found himself in the same situation as before, looking to release Toasters' music and no one to step up to the challenge. Again, Bucket turned to his D.I.Y. spirit. "We started Megalith in 2004, mainly because we wanted to put some Toasters records out and there was nobody to license them to. It's funny that we kind of returned to square one with how we started Moon, which is putting out Toasters records that nobody wanted to put out. It's funny how we came back to that and now we have forty releases and we're in the U.S.A. and Europe, so the snowball rolls down the hill again," says Bucket.

But things aren't exactly the same this time around. "What we're doing differently is basically letting it grow organically. So we're letting the label grow itself as opposed to putting it in places where it can't really support itself. With Moon we promoted it so much that the label got to be somewhere where it couldn't sustain itself and we're not going to let that happen with the new label," he says.

And Bucket himself has relocated, moving to Spain in 2004, meaning most all of the original members of the band continue to perform with other bands in New York. Today Bucket is the only original member of the Toasters who performs with the band, but he tours frequently in Europe and the U.S. It was a personal decision, he says. "I'm pretty New York, but one of the contributing factors was obviously 9–11 and re-evaluation and I just wanted to make a change and really have my kids get some European experience, that's a big thing. And with the success of the regime in New York of Giuliani and Bloomberg, for me they really destroyed the character of the city, turned it into a millionaire's playground and hell, they even allowed CBGBs to close. It has really just become a place that was familiar as a musician and had really lost all of its cutting edge. It was just a place where you just work for the man in New York now. That's not good enough for me," he says.

But Bucket wasn't the only early champion of ska in America. Also on the east coast, in Boston, a band called Bim Skala Bim began just after the Toasters formed in 1983. "The Toasters and Bim Skala Bim are definitely the two oldest American ska bands," says Jim Arhelger, drummer for Bim Skala Bim. When Jim Jones, guitar player for Bim Skala Bim, moved to Los Angeles, Arhelger later moved to Colorado in 2005, and singer Dan Vitale moved to Panama, it signaled the end of the band, although in 2010 they gathered again for a few reunion shows in Boston.

Arhelger says Bim Skala Bim picked up much of their sound from not only the 2Tone bands, but also the Jamaican greats with whom they regularly performed.

> The band is influenced by the older-style ska. We love the older stuff that came out of Jamaica that sort of became reggae. We're all huge fans of old reggae from especially the '70s and early '80s, when it was really good singers and actual bands rather than synthesizers and drum machines. Specific people, we were very influenced by Bob Marley definitely. The Skatalites. We played a couple of shows with Prince Buster when we were over in England. Bad Manners, one of the English ska bands, we're really huge fans of them. The Specials. Another reggae band, Black Uhuru, we love them. And also just tons of other music, rock music. I mean there's big rock influence in our music. We don't play much real traditional ska, it's just a jumping off point for us. We're kind of a ska rock band I guess you could say. We actually do a lot of really faster stuff. We don't do a lot of traditional one-drop ska beat.

Even though they may not characterize themselves as traditional, Bim Skala Bim did perform with traditional artists, like Prince Buster, as well as the Skatalites. Arhelger says:

> They got back together after a lot of years of not playing together, it was probably '86 or '87 and we did some shows with them and they were just incredibly friendly and Roland Alphonso played on our second album. That was really cool. *Tuba City* which came out in '87. We had

our album all done and we had a couple of spaces where there was room for him to play sax on. Actually, we took our tape down to Coxsone Dodd's studio down in Brooklyn, Studio One. He was very cool. We went down to his place in Brooklyn. Roland lived in Brooklyn and we went and picked him up at his apartment and took him down to the studio and got him lunch and stuff and he was just happy to be out playing. He was just an incredibly friendly funny, generous old guy. They just thought it was so cool that younger bands were picking up the torch and carrying it on. We knew we were around history.

Other bands too found their inspiration in the Jamaican greats, such as New York-based band the Scofflaws, who got their start in 1985. The band still performs live, although they haven't released a studio album since 1998. Buford O'Sullivan, who played trombone with the band until 2000 when he then went to perform with the Toasters and established a solo career, says the Scofflaws sound was set firmly in the Jamaican roots, blended with other non-ska genres for an individual flavor. O'Sullivan recalls:

It was the music the guys in the band were listening to, along with other kinds. They were very much into the rocksteady old school singer. The genre was very attractive to them. At the same time they were also listening to James Brown and Johnny Cash, so it has to do with good songs, and they were mixing it together. So they would listen to Prince Buster and Desmond Dekker, definitely. Sammy, Richie Brooks, we call him Sammy, is very into the Desmond Dekker-style of performance. You get up there, you do your moves and you kind of schmooze it and you have the facial expressions and you're looking sexy and all that kind of stuff, and that's always been there in ska. The singer gets up and has got to strut his stuff and sing. The sound system is going behind him and he's got to sing.

And O'Sullivan too, as a trombonist, traditionally one of the most important members of a ska band, stood upon the shoulders of the giants who came before him. "I've always been influenced by the instrumentalists. I'm the trombone player and I heard Don Drummond and Rico. I heard Rico in the Specials and then I heard Don Drummond in the Skatalites. I was amazed that a trombone player could be a star, because that's what Don Drummond was. He was the guy who could get up there, play a solo and get the entire crowd going. I mean people in Jamaica knew who Don Drummond was. He was very big. I heard that and thought, 'Oh, so I guess a guy can show himself on that horn,'" says O'Sullivan.

The Scofflaws began performing with the Toasters and other New York ska bands, establishing an east coast stronghold.

> The Scofflaws opened for the Toasters in '85 at CBGBs and it would be like the Scofflaws, the Boilers, the Toasters, maybe Urban Blight playing a show at CBGBs and it was a very selective, small scene. Everyone knew each other. And Buck, being a smart man, decided to get a label together, put his own records out, and start a business. And he started putting bands out and compilations. Still in '89 we were still playing and the Boilers had broken up and Skinnerbox is playing, Urban Blight stopped being hard core ska, and bands like Mephiskapheles were starting up, and in '92, '93 the Insteps formed and people were going to the shows and seeing it was working and the enthusiasm built. Family trees intermingle and bands breakup and re-form, people leave one thing and go to another.

Soon ska bands were springing up all over the country, blending their tastes for Jamaican and English ska with funk, soul, jazz, rock, and pop. Kids who heard 2Tone on their college radio station or through an older sibling grew keen to the sound and went straight from their school marching band to the stage. In 1986, California-based Let's Go Bowling began in this manner, forming out of another band, the Kyber Rifles. The band still performs today on the West Coast. Mark Michel founded the band and played bass, carrying on the tradition of ska after first hearing the English version:

> I had a buddy in junior high when we were in seventh grade. He had an older brother that was going to college at Cal, and he used to go visit him every so often and his brother would take him out, take him to shows, and I think it was in '81, English Beat was playing and he took him to the show and my buddy was just so blown away. He came back with their first album and said, "Hey, I got this cool music, listen to this," and so it was like, "Oh wow." Just from having heard the name, he's like, "Oh, here's the Specials, try this album too, oh wow!" So here we are in junior high, '81, '82 getting exposed to that. It was the Beat, the Specials, the Selecter and all that because when you first get into it,

that's the easiest because it's catchy and lively, and then if you're concerned enough to check the roots out you think, well this whole first Madness album, and this Specials album, they're covers and who did those tunes originally and then you go back and listen [Michel says].

Let's Go Bowling's popularity took band members all over the world to perform, frequently playing on the same bill as their childhood idols. "To be able to tour with those guys, especially the Specials, and sit up and talk to them every night, 'What does this song mean?' 'Well when I wrote this song, I got stabbed by a couple of racist skinheads,' talking to Lynval Golding. It's like, 'Wow,' playing with our idols. Every night you found yourself side stage watching the show," says Michel.

But this band, like so many other bands, and so many fans, used those roots to form their own brand of ska. Michel says, "The music branched out. There's the punk ska thing, the swing ska, all these different sounds, you have the skater kids, the surf kids, the normal kids that just listen to regular alternative instead of just that straight traditional or 2Tone sound, because it's something they can relate to. Instead of just liking one style, they'll like all the styles."

And shaping ska into an individual sound is not only American, but it is also evolution. Let's Go Bowling's Michael Rey de Leon explains, "We want to see what we can do with it and go for it and put it one stretch farther. I think we all want to be innovators here. We want to innovate the music. We don't want to be a really good ska band, we want to be a really good band, because if we're a really good ska band, we're not helping the genre at all. The innovators bring something new to the genre. We want to stretch it out, take it to another level. It's evolution. Take steps in leaps and bounds, not a little bit at a time."

The way most successful ska bands took the music to the next level and evolved the genre was to do what they knew and do what they did best — combining the ska sounds with other sounds they were skilled at playing. One of the most influential American ska bands that combined ska with a kaleidoscope of other styles, grew the genre of ska by influencing numerous others. Fishbone began playing their special brew in L.A. in 1979, founded by a group of friends in junior high school. One of those founding members, Angelo Moore, also known as Dr. Madd Vibe, is still vocalist and saxophone player for the band. He says he, like most other American ska musicians, was influenced by the ska coming from England. "What I was listening to at the beginning was, as far as ska goes, the Specials, Selecter, and Madness, Bodysnatchers, Bad Manners, people like that. And then after that, I started catching on to Jamaican ska, Toots & the Maytals and the Skatalites, even though Jamaican ska came before the England movement. That's the way I caught it. I caught it like that. This was like junior high school, like 1979, 1980, around that time," Moore says.

So the band took that sound and mixed it with a variety of other

genres, including funk, soul, R&B, punk, and hard rock. Moore says, "I'm in a band that plays ska, as well as. You know? Because the ska that we play, and almost all the other stuff that we play, everything is funk based. Everything is funk based, everything is soulful. Even if it's going a million miles an hour. If it's punk rock, then it's got a little gospel thing in it because it's the same tempo. A lot of fast gospel and punk rock have got the same tempo goin' on, different attitudes. Those two things, they've got in common the tempo, and I just put a lot of my soul and stuff into the punk rock, which gives it that really edgy psycho gospel."

Fishbone front man Angelo Moore, better known as Dr. Madd Vibe, has performed since 1979 with the band he founded in southern California. His blend of ska, soul, funk, and theater have influenced hundreds of bands (photograph Heather Augustyn).

But that eclectic blend wasn't always an easy sell to the music industry. Although Fishbone had great success through the '80s, touring with the Beastie Boys, filming a video directed by Spike Lee, performing on *Saturday*

184

Night Live, and scoring hits on MTV, they had their contract dropped by Sony in 1994, another contract dropped by Hollywood Records in 2000, and had a series of tough album sales in the later '90s and in the new millennium. Moore explains:

It's challenging because America as a country and the whole music industry, especially the way music is now, it's very linear in America. People listen to like one type of music, one language, and because it's one language, well, it's kind of like in America there's one way of thinking, money's one color, and that has a lot to do with how people think. And then of course, there's the music. You don't have a lot of different styles in America, at least that are exposed to the masses like you would have in Europe, so it makes it a little more challenging, especially if you're playing a lot of different styles. If you're playing one style or two styles, it's a lot easier for people to digest what you're doing because there's not a lot of color and flavor. I think ska is a tough sell in the U.S. because it's not pop. It's gotten a little closer to the mainstream, with Gwen Stefani and the Mighty Mighty Bosstones and Fishbone, but other than that, it's not like a generic rocker and R&B type of shit you listen to.

Even though Fishbone may not be played in rotation on radio stations, the band continues to perform to huge crowds all over the world and they collaborate with many other musicians, such as Outkast, Gwen Stefani, Primus, George Clinton, Donny Osmond, Rick James, and H.R. of Bad Brains. Through these collaborations, Fishbone is able to reach new audiences. "It's part of the musical flavor because Fishbone is really eclectic as opposed to being linear, like the country that we live in, the musical thinking and things like that, so if we're really eclectic in our music and subject matter, I think we're really going to draw a wide range of people. I think we give to our audience a sense of being, a sense of awareness that there is a bunch of color and a plethora of musical styles you can partake from," Moore says.

Fishbone has inspired others through their reach into other varieties of music over their long history. Aside from influencing non-ska bands, such as the Red Hot Chili Peppers, Living Colour, and 311, Fishbone has also inspired countless ska bands such as Sublime and, says Jayson Nugent of the Slackers, his own repertoire. "I grew up in Queens and moved downtown to go to school when I was 17. Friends of mine were starting a ska band. I didn't really know ska, but I knew Fishbone and stuff like that, and like reggae, so I thought sure, I'll give it a try. We started a band called Agent 99 in 1993," says Nugent.

Moore recognizes numerous musicians have been impacted by their funky brand of ska. For them, he offers some advice that speaks to the music industry as well. "Keep integrity to your music. Don't be lightin' their ass. Don't be lightin' their ass. You want to have music that's true to your heart, not where you feel like you're making the music for the money and you're just sorry they're playing that weak shit on the radio later on. Make the music that makes you feel good, something you can believe in."

Fishbone continues to offer their music to old audiences and new audiences alike. "I've thought about, why do we keep playing this music while others are dying around us [laughs]. We've had our ups and downs. I guess I just keep thinking it's the thing we do really good. Sure we can do more, but I guess the way the good lord has bestowed upon us, it's one of the only things we've been blessed with, to do, so I guess that's it. It's in the stars and all that. It's like a Rolling Stones phenomenon, I guess," says Moore.

Also hailing from the west coast, ska musicians Joey Altruda and Willie McNeil flavored their ska with an eclectic mixture of swing, lounge, and Latin. The fusion which became the trademark sound of Jump with Joey was a natural outcome of Altruda's and McNeil's environment. Altruda says:

> I was born and raised here in southern California and I grew up partially around the beach area and at the time I was a teenager, Poncho Sanchez and his group played a lot around where I was growing up, and he was friends with my older sister. Those were the times when Poncho Sanchez was playing also in Cal Tjader's band. Cal Tjader was a very Latin jazz player in the '50s to the '70s. He's still legendary. Being brought up also in San Gabriel, which is near east L.A., I had a lot of Mexican music around me, and different Latino music. It was a big Mexican culture and population in the town I grew up in. And being at the beach where I heard this music of Cal Tjader and people, it was a real influence. Then in '89, I started a Cuban jam session every Tuesday for five years and it was then I started learning about Cuban music and the structures of it and how it's played and the history of it. And at the same time, Willie

was also learning the same thing. We were playing at the same club and the Latin flavor just crept into our sound. It was never really a conscious decision to put it in. It just naturally evolved.

Willie McNeil, who grew up in Topeka, Kansas, had a background more typical of American ska bands, but when he met Altruda, the fusion was formed. "I got into it back in '79 when I got turned on to the Specials. I liked Madness and stuff back in the day but then I got more into dub and reggae cause at that time there was a lot of great dub going on. Once I moved to L.A. a friend of ours turned us on to a whole bunch of great classic ska, like early Prince Buster and all that kind of stuff. I used to have this one single back in the day, the A side was El Pussy Cat and the B side was Phoenix City and it was Roland Alphonso's single, and I used to love that fuckin' single, but I didn't really get into the depths of it until I moved to L.A. years later," McNeil says.

So Altruda, an upright bass player, and McNeil, a drummer, collaborated first in a band called Tupelo Chain Sex, and then in July 1989 as part of the seven-piece Jump with Joey. "We had a love for ska and that became part of our sound," says Altruda. But the audience their music appealed to was larger than ska fans alone because of their Latin vibe. "We weren't a typical 'ska' group with the two tone outfits and pork pie hats," says McNeil. The band broke up in 1999 and both Altruda and McNeil continue to perform independently. Altruda was musical director for L.A.'s legendary King King night club from 1988 to 1994, Club Bordello for its first 18 months of rebirth (2007–2008), and currently spends most of his time in Shanghai, working as musical director of China's premier cabaret club, Chinatown. His dedication to the music of Jamaica garnered a lifetime achievement award (2006) for his contribution to Jamaican music and culture. Says Altruda, "This music never goes out of style; it's always been in style."

While Jump with Joey may have developed ska along the lines of Latin, and Fishbone may have developed ska along the lines of funk, punk, and hard rock, others brought ska back along more traditional routes by invoking the roots of jazz. Fred Reiter, better known to fans and fellow musicians as Rocksteady Freddie, studied jazz at an early age, many years before he went to perform as saxophonist for the Toasters and the New York Ska Jazz Ensemble. "When I grew up, I went to East

187

Meadow High School, which is out on Long Island, and it had a really strong jazz ensemble and I was an all-state jazz player and performed with some well-known people. In college I used to play a lot of classical flute," says Reiter, who graduated from Princeton University.

Reiter, who was aware of Jamaican ska and reggae, then learned how to perform the genre after joining a ska band called the New York Citizens. "I was freelancing around New York and I got a call from my buddy to sub for a band called the New York Citizens and at the time they were a set unit and were really skeptical about having somebody just sort of do the show. And I was really interested in traveling and this buddy told me he was going all over with them, so I said, the next time, call me, and I made sure I really knew their stuff," says Reiter, who got the job.

But it wasn't long before Reiter got a more permanent post as saxophonist in a band that really would take him places — the Toasters. "It just turns out we, the New York Citizens, were opening up for the Toasters at Maxwell's in Hoboken. At the time they only had trombone and trumpet and I thought I could fit in really well with the band and I ended up speaking with Buck, the guitarist from the Toasters, and one thing led to another and in the course of maybe three or four months they gave me a shot to play one weekend, and from then on in, I was in the band," Reiter says.

He very quickly learned how to play ska, which he had not played during his rigorous jazz schooling. "Even though I was aware of ska and reggae as early as the '70s, because I had seen the Jimmy Cliff movie and I really dug the music and Desmond Dekker, it wasn't until later when I started doing the Citizens and the Toasters, I mean once I was in the Toasters, I was listening to ska bands every night, so I pretty much got a quick education," says Reiter.

That serious education included performing alongside the Jamaican and English pioneers that Reiter grew up listening to. He says, "I've been fortunate to play with a lot of talented people. I've played on stage with the Skatalites. It was a thrill. The real thrill was the first Skavoovie tour in '94 which was a major outing. We traveled around the country with the Skatalites, the Special Beat, and the Selecter and three of the Skatalites were all on our bus and I got to hang real heavy with those guys.

And it was actually the seedling of that tour that got us thinking about Ska Jazz, from going out and seeing the Skatalites all the time, and they're old Jamaican guys, but they were also brought up, they're basically jazz Jamaican guys so we had sort of the same musical upbringing. We know all of the same standards and stuff, so that was really cool, and I've been buddies with all those guys," says Reiter.

So Reiter began the New York Ska Jazz Ensemble to play a more jazz-infused style of ska. Of course he called upon his work with the Skatalites as a source into which he could tap, for talent and for inspiration. "I got Tommy McCook to play on the first Ska Jazz record. Tommy's real cool. He listens to a lot of Coltrane. He's always looking for that song that's going to put it over the edge. I call the Skatalites my fathers. They're the fathers of the ska movement. A lot of the kids that are growing up today on all the ska punk really don't know what ska is, let alone that it started in Jamaica. So ultimate respect to those guys. They got this beat going, the ska rhythm, and they played their jazz over it, which is similar to what we do, in a way, but we're trying to stretch that as well," Reiter says.

Cary Brown, keyboardist for the New York Ska Jazz Ensemble, also spent much of his time learning from the masters of ska before he put his own fingerprint on the genre. Brown performed keyboards for the Skatalites themselves. "When it was at its best, it felt just like being completely lifted up by the music. That's the only word I can think of to describe it is 'lift.' I, a few times, felt like I was being physically lifted up and moved by it just because they get going on this rhythm. That's what people love it for. It's got this lift and you feel transported. At times too, like with the way they play on their album, sometimes it's a bit more conservative, but when they really feel on, sometimes they really start to improvise too because they're all jazz musicians, and so sometimes I would feel like I was in Duke Ellington's band or something. What was going on, it was never just Jamaican music anymore because those guys have such jazz backgrounds," he says.

Brown got to know the members of the Skatalites personally as well as professionally, which translated into a music of his own. Brown recalls, "Hours and hours in the tour van. I definitely tried to cultivate a relationship with every one of them. Lloyd Knibb and I used to ride in his car because when I lived in Boston, he and I would drive together from Boston to whatever jobs we had, so he and I got to know each other really well. I wouldn't say it was culture shock, but you find they're coming from an extremely different place from where I grew up. Just their way of looking at things or expressing themselves, it took me a while just to understand their accents and stuff. As I got to know them, they're very open guys, very passionate guys."

On stage, Brown was a member of the band, just like the others, but they all recognized who was boss. "Tommy was the organizer of the group and was very particular about things. Tommy would never hesitate to turn around and say something to me on stage. It wasn't as if there was any doubt in anyone's mind who was calling the shots. Everyone had completely made the decision to leave it up to Tommy. He was a very strong leader that way. If he didn't like the rhythm or something, he would body motion or say something verbally and people would definitely listen to him," Brown says.

That musical direction, Brown brought with him to the New York Ska Jazz Ensemble. He and Reiter, as well as other ska musicians, comprised the band. Today, many of these musicians rotate in and out as their schedules permit with the band's tour schedule. "They wanted to grow into the jazz side of it, just like I did," says Brown, who was classically trained in piano. Reiter says the focus on jazz was a natural progression. "For me, what Ska Jazz has done is try to meld them in a way that hasn't been done before. Myself and Rick Faulkner, the trombonist from the Toasters, simultaneously came up with this idea that we also would like to stretch out a bit and blow a little bit more, and we thought of all these guys, especially the ones we met on the Skavoovie tour, like Cary Brown, and Victor [Rice], formerly of the Scofflaws, and basically it started off as a musical endeavor to try some different kinds of tunes, try some different writing, different styles," Reiter says.

Although Hepcat may be a little less jazz than New York Ska Jazz Ensemble, they still perform in the more traditional vein of ska. "Part of the reason we started the band is cause we'd get mad when we'd go to ska shows and the music they were playing between the bands was more interesting than the actual bands," says Hepcat's vocalist, Alex Desert. The band still performs together and Desert also has a successful acting career, on movies such as *Swingers*, television shows such as *Becker* and *Boy Meets World*, and even video games such as the *Tomb Raider* series.

Hepcat's traditional sound stemmed from the musicians' background that was similar to the Jamaican pioneers. "Jazz is a big influence for us. Jazz and I'd say soul music, like old R&B from the '50s. If you listen to our harmonies, there's a lot of far-out stuff, like Earth, Wind, and Fire. We figured if we were going to do the old school we should have our roots be deeply rooted in the old school," says Desert. And performing properly, says Desert, isn't as simple as it seems. "People think ska is easy, but it's not, if you get it right. It's easy to play ska, but it's hard to play good ska. That's the difference, and even the best jazz musician won't grasp the concept. They think everything is two and four, real easy," he says.

The thought that ska was easy to play led to the creation of hundreds of ska bands all over the nation, and all over the world. But the glut of bands crashed the industry without producing any hugely successful ska bands, unless their crossover appeal was strong. Bands like No Doubt, Sublime, and the Mighty Mighty Bosstones were able to find success beyond most others. No Doubt's blend of white suburban ska and pop brought the band's four members, Gwen Stefani, Tony Kanal, Adrian Young, and Tom Dumont, 27 million records sold worldwide to date. Formed in Anaheim, California, in 1986, the band has collaborated with many Jamaican artists, including Sly & Robbie, and they have two Grammy awards.

No Doubt bassist Tony Kanal says:

Ska and reggae music are the foundation of our band and continue to guide our musical explorations to this day. In our formative years, we were hugely influenced by both the British 2Tone ska movement and the reggae bands that emerged from England in the late '70s and early '80s. Bands like Madness, the Specials, the Selecter, the English Beat, UB40, and Steel Pulse all had a huge impact on us. Our early set lists always included cover songs like "Baggy Trousers" [Madness] and "Gangsters" [the Specials] and even as recently as 2004, we played "All I Want To Do" [UB40] and "Racist Friend" [the Special A.K.A.] in our live show. While our sound has obviously grown and expanded over the years, these original influences retain an incredibly important place in our musical world.

When No Doubt began in 1986, southern California had a thriving underground ska and mod scene which we became a part of. It was this community of bands, fans and lifestyle that enabled our growth as a band and built our fan base during our early years. While there were many great "traditional" ska bands that were part of this scene, there were also bands such as Fishbone and the Untouchables who were pushing ska and reggae into different directions. We obviously gravitated more towards this approach.

The Mighty Mighty Bosstones, an eight-piece ska band hailing from Boston, also met with great success by blending ska with hardcore punk and hard rock for a concoction labeled ska-core. Their album *Let's Face It* on Mercury Records went platinum and the single off of the album, "The Impression That I Get," went to number one on Modern Rock charts. The group formed in 1985. Lead Vocalist Dicky Barrett remembers how they first were introduced to the ska sound at a young age in Boston.

> As far as the Jamaican ska, roots and reggae pioneers go, we discovered that stuff after falling in love with the English 2Tone movement, mostly because we grew up in Boston in the Eighties and Nineties. We kind of had the cart out in front of the horse, but what are you going to do? I'm sure there are baby ska bands and fans these days dusting off some now classic Specials disc because they really got into ska when they heard one of our songs. Whatever it takes to keep it alive. My road to discovering all things ska began when I saw the English Beat open up for the Pretenders in Boston in 1980 I think. My mind was completely blown by Roger, Dave, and the lads. The next day I bought every ska and 2Tone record my local record store had to offer. I was crazy about the Specials and loved the Selecter, but Madness were my absolute favorites. I can't talk about English second wave without mentioning Bad Manners. We loved Buster and his crew a whole lot as well. From there I started doing my homework and discovered the magical, musical wonders of such first wave Jamaican artists as Prince Buster and the Skatalites. It's a fairly common third waver saga.

He describes the special Bosstones blend as a mixture of the group's interests. He says, "We were Boston street punks when we were kids, and part of the American hardcore scene so of course we incorporated that into what it was we were doing. We hooked up with some decent musicians early on who were influenced by a lot of jazz so we threw that in. I have always loved '70s AM radio music so there's some of that corniness in there as well. We've never limited ourselves and we love and we're influenced by all types of music, except turn of the century sea shanties."

Barrett says since they formed in 1985, a lot has changed in the ska scene, but a lot has also remained the same and the common thread is the music's message. "Subcultures change with trends and culture in general. I think ska music has always been very honest music, and very often lyrically insightful (for the most part). It has always been historically political on some level. So the time and place the ska music is being made should be heavy factors. The music and message a Kingston guy makes in the early '60s is going to be different than that of a London guy in the early '80s which will be different from the music a Bostonian is going to make in the '90s. Making ska music when President Obama is in office is going to be a lot different than making it during the eight years that George Bush ran the country. You watch," says Barrett.

Ska punk band Sublime also capitalized on the West Coast trend in the 1990s with a blend called skacore and sold 17 million albums worldwide.

In the Midwest, still a force in Chicago and around the globe is Deal's Gone Bad, a band that combines ska with soul. But that sound evolved, says guitarist Dave Simon.

> We started in 1994 and I was into 2Tone and some old Jamaican stuff, but I was more into the rocksteady. We've gone through a lot of different people and the people that started off in the beginning were a bunch of 2Tone punk kids and as we were losing and firing people throughout the years, we were getting people who were more into rocksteady and soul music. A lot of the skinheads I was hanging out with were listening to rocksteady and soul. Jackie Wilson, Otis Redding, Sam & Dave. Once we got Todd Hembrook in the band, he has a very powerful soul voice, he can sing that real well, so we can play rocksteady with a lot of soul emphasis. The vocals are more Sam & Dave and the horns are even — well back when we first started, the horn would play a real lot and now it's like some songs don't have much horn at all, or a little tag. It's not about horns anymore. I think it's like a three minute rocksteady soul song.

Simon says the meaning of their songs, which address real everyday issues such as relationships, is what has led to their popularity all over the world. "We think about different things, since we're from Chicago. Part of all of that soul impression came from Chicago. I love the way it's become more song writing instead of 'check out what I can do.' It's more important to get into the song. We've been to Turkey, Slovenia, Romania, Macedonia. We've been to France and Germany and people are really into it and there are skinheads everywhere we go. Fans are awesome. Some we played at a big fest with thousands of people. Some were smaller. But the people are really into it. Some of our songs have a lyric in there that people will hear and say, 'Oh, that's how I feel.' It's a little more personal. It's not about drinking a beer or riding the bus," Simon says.

With the exception of a handful of strong bands that still survive today, the American ska industry collapsed at the turn of the millennium. The Slackers' Jayson Nugent remembers:

> Around 2000 or so, the ska scene was building throughout the '90s, and around 2000 it collapsed because there were so many more people in ska bands than there were buying the records. The records weren't selling and everyone was in a ska band. Everyone in a high school marching band had a band, so there were just too many bands with too many people in it and nobody's actually buying the records. It collapsed and believe it or not, that actually helped the Slackers because it really weeded out all the suckers. A lot of people had, and still have, really bad connotations of it. In all honesty, a lot of ska bands really sucked. Not to say we're better than them. A lot of them just really draw weak influences and copy what everyone else is doing. They don't have the tradition in it, not that it should just be retro music, but there's just nothing new out there. I can understand why a lot of people don't like ska. It actually helped us when the ska scene fell off. We actually did way better as a band. Moon Records is a perfect example. They put out every record from every band. They didn't sell enough records. You have to turn a profit at the end of the day.

Isaac Green, founder and occasional back-up vocalist for the band Isaac Green and the Skalars, concurs. "It just sort of broke down," says Green of the ska industry. "Moon epitomized a scene label, where with each new round of artists, they all sold less. There were more artists that sold less copies of each record. The first round with Let's Go Bowling and Dance Hall Crashers and Hepcat and the Toasters and The Pietasters, they sold a lot. And we were in the second round with Spring Heeled Jack and Skavoovie & the Epitones. We sold decently and then it kept getting smaller with each new round of bands," Green says. Today, Green has established his own record label, Starlight International, and has the perspective of hindsight as well as professional knowledge to assess the flaws of the ska business.

> You have to focus on bands [he says]. Is this band someone's favorite band, not is this band someone they would enjoy dancing to on a Saturday night along with five other bands? That's the biggest thing. I think there are a number of really good albums that came out of that era, and hundreds of bad ones. But I still love listening to the Pietasters and I'm a really big Slackers fan. They made really good records, so the music lasts longer. It was hard making records in that time because the bands were very young. They had a very unwieldy recording setup, more than just guitar, bass, and drums. They were working with tiny budgets and very inexperienced people. Maybe later, Hepcat, maybe the Slackers, Pietasters, and Toasters could record in a way that was highly professional. They set the path. Certain bands can definitely make records very cheap that sound great, but it's tough when you're so young.
>
> None of the bands were able to grab the sort of national consciousness to really push them over the top, to really set the ska movement in shape, because it stayed niche the whole time, even though it was a big niche. All those Jamaican artists had huge hit singles. Even the best American ska bands weren't even coming close, unless you count No Doubt, and you can include the Mighty Mighty Bosstones. Great songs carry over for years and years and become part of your life and your memories. Not-great songs don't.

But Green, as well as many other bands, and even more fans, remains optimistic about the future of ska in America. "It could come back, you just need a couple of great bands. It can't be another hundred mediocre bands," he says. And with the continued success of modern ska bands who refuse to pack it in, and the English and Jamaican artists who continue to tour all over the world to record numbers of fans, despite losing band members to sickness or even death, ska is something that will be a part of the musical fabric of the world forever. And the reach is global. Barrett says, "It seems to be loved and respected almost every-where — Japan, Germany, all over South America, where we should prob-ably play some day. I think people the world over love ska music, especially when the Mighty Mighty Bosstones play it, because it's good."

Bucket, who has hitched his wagon to the ska star for three decades, says he thinks ska is simply becoming better with age. "Ska music is back in the underground, which is a good thing and I think now we're seeing that we're going to have the opportunity to grow a whole new generation of grassroots bands. Ultimately, even though the money is not there, that's bad for some bands and depressing for touring, but ulti-mately it's good for the style, and really that's the most important thing. The music is way more important than the bands that play it," he says. Bucket truly epitomizes the dedication to ska music that so many per-formers and listeners possess. "This is real music, real people. Roots and culture."

Bibliography

Aitken, Laurel. Interview, July 6, 1997.

Alphonso, Roland. Interview, May 17, 1997.

Altruda, Joey. Interview, July 11, 1997; emails to author, November 3, 2008, March 19, 2010.

Arhelger, Jim. Interview, April 16, 1997.

Bad Manners: Don't Knock the Bald Heads. Mvd Visual, 2005, DVD.

Barrett, Dicky. Email to author, November 19, 2008.

Barrow, Steve. "Tougher Than Tough: The Story of Jamaican Music" [CD booklet]. London: Mango Records, 1993.

Bradley, Lloyd. *This Is Reggae Music: The Story of Jamaica's Music.* New York: Grove Press, 2000.

Brevett, Lloyd. Interview, May 17, 1997.

Brown, Cary. Interview, April 13, 1997.

Bushell, Garry. "Rude Boys Can't Fail." *Sounds,* March 15, 1980.

Buster, Prince. Interview, July 14, 1997.

Byers, Roddy. Emails to author, March 7, 2008, July 3, 2008, July 23, 2008, August 27, 2008, March 15, 2010.

Chambers, Pete. "You're wondering now!" *Backbeat,* February 8, 2005.

Charlery, Roger. Interview, June 27, 1997.

Clarke, Sebastian. *Jah Music: The Evolution of the Popular Jamaican Song.* London: Heinemann Educational Books, 1980.

Clayden, Andy. "Madness Story." www.dangermen.net/MadnessStory/madness.htm (accessed January 5, 2009).

Dammers, Jerry. "The Specials Madness and the rise and fall of 2-Tone." *Uncut,* July 1998.

de Koningh, Michael, and Laurence Cane-Honeysett. *Young, Gifted and Black: The Story of Trojan Records.* London: Sanctuary House, 2003.

de Leon, Michael Rey. Interview, July 28, 1997.

Desert, Alex. Interview, June 22, 1997.

Du Noyer, Paul. "The Specials: Ending of An Era?" *New Musical Express*, August 8, 1981.

Foster, Chuck. *Roots Rock Reggae: An Oral History of Reggae Music from Ska to Dancehall*. New York: Billboard Books, 1999.

_____. *The Small Axe Guide to Rock Steady*. London: Muzik Tree & I Am the Gorgon, 2009.

Green, Isaac. Interview, November 3, 2008.

Halasa, Malu. *The Beat: Twist and Crawl*. Richmond, U.K.: Eel Pie, 1981.

Hasted, Nick. "Jerry Dammers: A Ghost from the Past." Independent.co.uk, April 20, 2007.

Hebdige, Dick. *Cut 'n' Mix: Culture, Identity and Caribbean Music*. London: Routledge, 1987.

Hibbert, Frederick. Interview, February 8, 2008.

Hingley, Robert. Interviews, April 11, 1997, November 29, 2008.

Hughes, Alex. Interview, June 22, 1997.

Isler, Scott. "2Tone: A Checkered Past" [CD booklet]. London: Chrysalis Records, 1993.

Kanal, Tony. Email to author, February 1, 2010.

Katz, David. *Solid Foundation: An Oral History of Reggae*. New York: Bloomsbury, 2003.

Keyo, Brian. "Foundation Ska: A Brief History of the Skatalites" [CD booklet]. Boston: Heartbeat Records, 1996.

Knibb, Lloyd. Interview, May 17, 1997.

Laurel Aitken and Friends, Live at Club Ska. Cherry Red UK, 2005, DVD.

Madness Central. "Madness In Print: 30 Years of Words and Pictures." www.madnesstradingring.com/InPrint/InPrint.html (accessed January 5, 2009).

Madness Information Service. "The Nutty Boys Madness Comix." No.1, January 1, 1981.

Marshall, George. *Spirit of '69: A Skinhead Bible*. Edinburgh: S.T. Publishing, 1994.

McNeil, Willie. Interview, July 31, 1997; email to author, October 31, 2008.

Michel, Mark. Interview, July 28, 1997.

Miles, Barry. *The 2-Tone Book for Rude Boys*. London: Omnibus Press, 1981.

Millar, Robbi. "No Surrender to Racism." *Sounds*, January 17, 1981.

Moore, Angelo. Interview, November 5, 2008.

Morgan, Derrick. Interview, June 5, 1997.

Nugent, Jayson. Interview, October 27, 2008.

O'Sullivan, Buford. Interview, March 31, 1997.

Rambali, Paul. "The Promised Land Calling." *New Musical Express*, February 1980.

Reiter, Fred. Interviews, April 11, 1997, May 10, 1997.

Robinson, Greg. "The Skatalites: Playing the Jamaican Sound." *Windplayer*, No. 51.

Shaffer, Doreen. Interviews, May 17, 1997, January 9, 2008.

Simon, Dave. Interview, March 16, 2010.

Sire Records Press Release, Madness Central. www.madnesstradingring.com/InPrint/1980/SireOneStepBeyondPR.html (accessed January 5, 2009).

Ska Explosion, Cleopatra, 1995, videocassette.

Small, Millie. Email to author, September 28, 2008.

Staple, Neville. Interview, July 9, 1997.

_____, and Tony McMahon. *Original Rude Boy*. London: Aurum Press, 2009.

Sterling, Lester. Recorded interview with author, May 17, 1997.

Sutherland, Steve. "Madness: The Life and Times of Britain's Nuttiest Band." *Melody Maker* (insert), 1983.

Taitt, Lyn. Interview, June 11, 2009.

The Harder They Come. Dir. Perry Henzell, Criterion, 2000, DVD.

Thompson, Dave. *Wheels Out of Gear: 2Tone, the Specials, and a World in Flame*. London: Helter Skelter, 2004.

Thompson, Lee. Email to author, October 23, 2008.

Todd, Millicent. Interview, March 3, 2009.

Trendle, Douglas. Interview, December 10, 2008.

Wakeling, Dave. Interview, January 29, 2008.

White, Timothy. *Catch a Fire*. New York: Henry Holt, 1983.

Williams, Mark. "Alpha Boys' School: Music in Education" [CD booklet]. London: Trojan, 2006.

_____. "Madness in the USA: That Heavy, Heavy Sound Arrests Manhattan." *Melody Maker*, March 15, 1980.

Williams, Paul. *You're Wondering Now: A History of the Specials*. Edinburgh: S.T. Publishing, 1995.

Index